Teen People®
real life diaries

OTHER Teen People® BOOKS:

LOVE STORIES

SEX FILES

Teen People
real life diaries

INSPIRING TRUE STORIES FROM
CELEBRITIES AND REAL TEENS

EDITED BY **LINDA FRIEDMAN** AND **DANA WHITE**

AVON BOOKS
AN IMPRINT OF HARPERCOLLINS*PUBLISHERS*

Contents

Letter from the EDITOR

"Reality" is pretty popular these days—from reality TV to true-confession talk shows to in-your-face live coverage of wars in distant places (or car chases on freeways in Los Angeles). We're bombarded with other people's life experiences that are supposedly uncensored and unfictionalized. Sometimes we can't take our eyes off the TV; other times it's all we can do to look.

In *Real Life Diaries*, *Teen People* offers you a different take on reality, one we think you'll approach with your eyes wide open. Three and a half years ago, when we started *Teen People*, a major part of our mission was to give real teens a big voice in the magazine. We wanted our readers—you—to be able to open the magazine and see yourself in its pages: your hopes, fears, triumphs, mistakes.

Some of the stories in *Real Life Diaries* were originally published in *Teen People* magazine; others were commissioned specifically for this book. Whether it's Aaron Carter describing what it's like to grow up in the shadow of a superstar brother, or the startling tale of two sisters who cut themselves, these first-person stories are direct, perceptive and above all, true. Hard lessons, small victories, enormous changes and tender realizations are threaded through with a ribbon of hope. It took honesty and sheer nerve to put most of these words on paper; those are qualities that characterize many of the stories you find in *Teen People* every month.

I hope you enjoy these slices of real life. Today, as some rappers have put it, it's all about "keepin' it real." This book is *Teen People*'s contribution to that goal—a collection of diaries that are about as real as you can get.

Barbara O'Dair
Managing Editor, *Teen People*

Carson Daly:

Soul Searcher

THE HOST OF MTV'S *TRL* TELLS OF THE
MOMENT HE DISCOVERED GOD, AND
HOW IT CHANGED HIS LIFE.

CARSON DALY
AS TOLD TO JENNIFER GRAHAM

ONE NIGHT IN FEBRUARY 1998, I WAS TERRIFIED TO DO SOMETHING: MY FIRST ON-AIR INTERVIEW FOR MTV.

The guest was Marilyn Manson, and I'd heard that he had a temperamental and explosive personality. How was I—Mr. Friendly VJ guy—going to handle this? I prepared by devouring his autobiography and reading every interview he had ever given. When I was through, I knew more about him than he did. But there was one more thing I needed to do: pray that I wouldn't blow it.

Thankfully, I didn't. And since then, I've gotten to know Marilyn pretty well—I really enjoy his company.

You don't believe that the host of MTV's *TRL* prays in stressful situations? Guess again. I've trusted my faith and leaned on it in tough times since my junior year of high school. My faith keeps my priorities in check: I wasn't put on this planet to look cool on TV. I'm here to live my life the best I can. For a short time, I even considered becoming a Catholic priest.

I'm sure it sounds like a big jump—from a man of the cloth to an MTV host, living in the fast lane. But I'm determined to stick by my convictions no matter what environment I'm in, and that includes the often-decadent music business. I don't mean to sound preachy; I'd NEVER push my beliefs on someone else. This is simply what I'm about.

> ## I don't mean to sound preachy; I'd NEVER push my beliefs on someone else. This is simply what I'm about.

When Carson got the job as host of MTV's *TRL*, it threw him smack in the middle of the often-decadent music business. Here he's seen with the group Next.

heaven SENT

I haven't always felt this way. Growing up, I fidgeted my way through Catholic church services with my mom, stepdad (my real dad died when I was five) and older sister, Quinn. I was a California kid from Santa Monica who loved skateboarding, surfing and golfing. Believe me, God wasn't high on my list of priorities. But that changed when I was seventeen.

I had been eating lunch with a bunch of friends at a local L.A. hangout, New York Pizza, in Westwood, when it happened. I remember my friend Ryan Morelli talking and then suddenly I felt a warm, comforting hand on my head. It stayed there for a good fifteen seconds. But when I looked around, no one was touching me. (I know this sounds freaky, but bear with me.) Then I started having hot flashes. My eyes began to burn, and I started to sweat. My mind started racing—I thought about how lucky I was to live in California, and to have such great friends and supportive parents. Then, unbelievably, my brain became awash with even bigger issues, like world poverty! All at once, I realized how much I had and how badly I wanted to use it to help others.

> **All at once, I realized how much I had and how badly I wanted to use it to help others.**

As soon as it was over, I walked straight over to the pay phone and called my mom. "Look, I'm not crazy," I began, "but I love you. And I just want to tell you right now, thank you for everything."

"Are you drunk?" she asked. I'm sure that's how I sounded. "You know our rule," she continued. "I'll come pick you up, no questions asked." As soon as I saw her, I told her everything. I explained how, for the first time, I realized that I owed somebody something for my life and all of the good things in it, that we didn't just spontaneously appear on earth. There are reasons for our lives. She didn't understand at first, but how could I blame her? I was confused myself.

I held off telling my friends. I could just imagine it:

"Hey, guys! I just got touched by something. I feel like a new man, and I love my mommy!" But as time went by, they couldn't help but notice a change in me. I began not just to obey my parents, but to talk to them honestly and openly. And, unlike a lot of guys my age, I refused to have meaningless hookups with girls.

Eventually, I told my friends everything, and they were all fine with it. I remember explaining to Ryan what really happened at the pizza place, and him saying, "That's really cool, man."

A year later, when I was a high school senior, entering a seminary was definitely on my mind. But so was golf—playing for the Santa Monica High School Vikings and practicing with UCLA's team, I ranked among the state's top high school golfers. When I was offered a partial golf scholarship to L.A.'s Loyola Marymount University, I decided to go, figuring I would major in theology.

> Unlike a lot of guys my age, I refused to have meaningless hookups with girls.

After a short time at Loyola, I left to attend College of the Desert in Palm Desert, California, and to pursue a pro golf career. (By then I had decided against the seminary, figuring I could apply my strong moral beliefs more effectively outside of the priesthood.) Once there, I ran into Jimmy Kimmel, a DJ at a local radio station and an old family friend. He got me an internship, then a salaried DJ job the following year, just as my pro golf plans were beginning to lose steam. Over the next four years, I did what many radio DJ's do: I moved from city to city, gradually taking jobs at bigger and bigger stations. By twenty-three, I'd relocated six times, ultimately landing at the most influential radio station in modern rock, L.A.'s KROQ [K-Rock]. I got to interview all the biggest names in music: Hole, Bush, No Doubt, Garbage, Oasis. Within a year, MTV called. That meant another move; this time, to New York to host my own TV show.

If K-Rock got my feet wet, this job hurled me full-throttle into the entertainment world—a place that's fun and glamorous, but not exactly morally sound. At MTV, I've seen the power that fame brings, and the mistakes I could

Though Carson's life hasn't been completely trouble free, he feels thankful for all that he has and now wants to give back to others. Here, he bats the ball around for kids at Arthur Ashe Kids' Day held in the USTA National Tennis Center, Flushing Meadows, New York, in 1998.

easily make with it. Young actresses and singers have politely sat through my interviews only to come on to me aggressively when the cameras went off. Backstage at concerts, groupies have offered me drugs, and attractive girls have suggested sex. It would be so easy to throw your morals out the window in times like these. But I've found that if you are strong, you'll be rewarded tenfold.

Leading a spiritual life, however, hasn't left me problem free. When my mom was diagnosed with breast cancer, it practically killed me. My first reaction was, God, please, what the hell is going on?! But I knew I had to let go. After thinking of all the reasons why I loved and needed her, I ultimately prayed that I would have the strength to deal with what was happening. My mom is fine now, but keeping my faith strong helped me get through that difficult time.

Because of my MTV exposure, I've had young viewers reach out to me. One thirteen-year-old girl wrote to me about how her older brother was beating her up. I figured that she probably hadn't let her parents in on this, but she was telling ME. So I called her. We talked it over, and I tried to explain the difference between roughhousing and real abuse. By the end of our conversation, I'd convinced her to tell her parents what was happening in a firm way that would make them listen. Her brother doesn't lay a hand on her now.

I've also tried to keep the moral bar high at MTV. One time, the producers wanted me to ask the audience, "When do you enjoy sex most: morning, afternoon or night?" But I was uncomfortable with that question; it assumes that all of our viewers—many of whom are just sixteen—are already having sex. That would make virgins uneasy. So instead, they let me ask the broader question "Do your male friends hook up more than your female friends do?"

That's just one example. But when I get discouraged about not doing enough, I look at it like this: As a priest, I might have touched a few hundred people. At MTV, I have the potential to reach so many more. I've been put here for a reason—this is where I need to be.

fast-forward

In February 1999, I wrote about my spirituality in the pages of *Teen People*. It was the only time I've shared something so personal. And I received my share of negative responses. You always do with a topic like spirituality. But it bothered me that some people accused me of preaching or telling them how to live their lives. That wasn't the case at all. I was just writing about *my* spirituality. I wasn't trying to convince people to get baptized. If you mention God in an article, inevitably somebody will call you a Jesus freak. Or they'll see you on a beach during spring break with a girl in a bikini and call you a hypocrite.

But overall, the response was positive. A lot of people were inspired by my story. And a few wrote and said they'd had similar experiences. I'm glad I shared this part of my life, because a lot of fans look up to me as a role model. If they see me embracing my spirituality, they might feel like it's okay for them to do the same. Many kids are ashamed to say they have a relationship with God. They think it's not cool. I'm glad I was able to help them see that it is.

> If you mention God in an article, inevitably somebody will call you a Jesus freak.

Ashley Rhodes-Courter:

Escape

from

Foster Care

NINE YEARS IN THE FOSTER CARE SYSTEM

COULD RUIN A KID. BUT THIS INDOMITABLE

TEEN NOT ONLY SURVIVED, SHE THRIVED.

NOW SHE SPEAKS OUT SO THAT OTHER KIDS

WON'T SUFFER AS SHE DID.

ASHLEY RHODES-COURTER
AS TOLD TO DANA WHITE

GROWING UP, I ALWAYS KNEW THAT MY LIFE WASN'T NORMAL. I ENTERED FLORIDA'S FOSTER CARE SYSTEM

when I was three and endured fourteen placements over the next nine years. (I had to make a spreadsheet recently to keep them straight.) When I was seven, my half brother and I lived with fourteen other kids in a trailer, where our foster parents physically and verbally abused us. But I tried not to think about what was happening to me. I knew the facts of my life, but I didn't really care to analyze them. There was no alternative, so why bother? Being in foster care kind of sucks the emotion out of you. Besides, I didn't want to feel sorry for myself—"oh, my mother gave me up, poor me." I was trying to make something of myself, and I knew that self-pity wasn't going to get me anywhere.

TEEN PEOPLE: Real Life Diaries

I was born in North Carolina in November 1985. My mother was only seventeen when she had me; I don't know who my father is. Three years later, my half brother, Jeremy, was born. He was very premature and spent the first nine months of his life in a hospital. Later my mom took us and moved to Florida. Unfortunately, she had a substance abuse problem and ended up getting arrested. In May 1989, when I was three, some people came and took Jeremy and me away from her. I spent the next two and a half years in five different foster homes. Sometimes Jeremy was in the same home, sometimes he wasn't. When I was five, "the system" sent us to live with my mother's father and his girlfriend on his farm back in North Carolina. My grandfather's girlfriend was a kind person, but my grandfather had problems with alcohol and violence. He'd drink too much and play chicken with his drunken neighbors with us in the car, which had no seat belts or doors. Finally, after my grandfather was wounded in a gunfight, Jeremy and I were removed from his home.

Over the next fifteen months I lived in two foster homes, and in June 1993, Jeremy and I ended up with Charles and Marjorie Moss, a middle-aged couple in Plant City, Florida. The Mosses lived in a blue trailer on a big piece of property in the middle

By the time she was four, Ashley had entered the foster care system and had lived in three different places.

My mother was only seventeen when she had me; I don't know who my father is.

Ashley Rhodes-Courter: Escape from Foster Care

of nowhere. Sixteen foster kids, from babies to teenagers, lived with them in that trailer. We slept in two bedrooms—girls in one room, boys in the other—in bunk beds stacked three levels high. Foster kids come with several hundred dollars a month, and kids like my brother who had special needs, such as a learning disability, came with even more. The Mosses were raking in the cash on us.

eight months
in hell

At first it seemed like just another placement. The Mosses were nice when a social worker was around, but I soon realized how heartless and cruel they really were. I remember I had been sick with the flu or something. Extremely nauseated, I rushed to the bathroom to throw up, but I didn't make it. Instead of comforting me, Miss Moss shoved my face into the puddle of vomit, just as you would a dog that had messed on the floor. She wanted me to call her "Mom."

The Mosses were crude people with wrinkly skin and bad teeth. While they sat on the couch watching TV and smoking, the kids took care of the household. We all had chores. My job, at seven years old, was taking care of the babies. I'd get up in the morning, change their diapers and give them breakfast. If a baby cried at night, I'd have to comfort it and I'd get in trouble if I couldn't quiet the baby down. At bath time, Miss Moss would fill the tub with about two inches of water. The babies bathed first, and the older kids had to use the same water, even if the babies had gone to the bathroom in it. If Miss Moss thought you hadn't taken a long enough bath, she'd scrub your entire body with a stiff bristle brush. The Mosses only changed the bed linens once a month, and if you wet the bed, you were stuck with those sheets. Once, after wetting my bed, I was forced to put

> My job, at seven years old, was taking care of the babies.

on one of the baby's diapers and go to each person in the trailer and say, "I'm sorry for pissing on myself. I'm a disgusting, filthy person."

We were punished if we used profanity, punished if we talked back, punished if we walked with the left foot instead of the right. The Mosses would slap us and hit us and throw us about. Some mornings they would lock us outside the trailer without food until nightfall, not even letting us back in to use the bathroom. They would force us to run laps around a cow pasture. I would run and run and run two miles or some ridiculous amount, without water, under a blazing sun. Once or twice Miss Moss sat me in a high chair and pinned my arms under the tray so they couldn't move. Then she'd force my head back and pour great quantities of hot sauce into my mouth. If I spit it out or worse yet swallowed it, she'd just pour more back in. Another time I was forced to squat underneath a low kitchen counter. I was supposed to hold that position, but it was awkward and difficult. I kept falling, so Miss Moss took a slotted spoon and beat my hide until it was completely raw. To keep from crying, I bit the inside of my mouth until I'd chewed open a big bloody hole in my cheek. That was enough to unnerve even Miss Moss, so she took me to the doctor, telling me to lie and say I'd fallen down the stairs. Many years later I read in a report that the official reason for my injury was "poor dental hygiene." Sometimes I allowed myself to dream of a better life. I'd imagine big houses with pools and animals and the prince on the white horse. But I knew life wasn't like that.

> Sometimes I allowed myself to dream of a better life.

ENOUGH Is Enough

I was the kind of kid who knew how to stay out of trouble, and eventually I learned how to avoid a lot of the punishment. My brother wasn't so lucky. Miss Moss would dunk his head in the toilet or the bathtub until he'd nearly drown. Jeremy got the hot-sauce punishment many more times than I did. I'll never forget standing there, watching my own brother endure that torture and being powerless to stop it.

I remember telling my social workers about what was happening to us. The Mosses were investigated, but it didn't go anywhere because most of the kids were too afraid to admit what was happening. I kept complaining, and eventually the Mosses got rid of Jeremy and me. Later I found out they were actually allowed to adopt eight of the children.

From there I was put in a shelter home called Lake Magdalene. I told everyone I came into contact with about what had happened to me at the Mosses', and finally one night a police officer came to question me about them. Otherwise, I don't remember anyone taking the initiative to do anything about them. After three months at Lake Magdalene, I was sent to live in a foster home where Jeremy had been placed. That lasted three months. Jeremy could be difficult to handle, and we were split up and sent to live in different foster homes. Unlike the Mosses, most of the homes were pretty normal family environments. I lived with nice people who took care of me as best they could, and that's about all I could really expect.

Sometimes I'd be driven to see my mother at the foster care headquarters in Tampa. Certain floors had visitation rooms where parents and kids would meet. We'd visit for an hour or so, and she'd give me presents. Once she brought me a wooden jewelry box with a little clock on the front and a lid with beautiful carved flowers. Other times she gave me shoes or an Easy-Bake oven. Then someone would come get me and drive me back to the foster home, my gifts on my lap.

RISING above it all

In 1994, when I was nine, my mother decided she'd never be able to take care of me, so she signed away her parental rights to me. (She'd signed away her rights to Jeremy

earlier.) I was now legally available for adoption.

In June 1995, we were placed in The Children's Home, a group facility in Tampa. I lived there for two and a half years. It was actually a nice place. There were six different "cottages" that housed twelve kids each. Every year The Home had the Murphy Award, a sort of mini Olympics where kids competed in events such as running and swimming. The house with the most points got the "house cup." The second year, I won three gold medals and was named outstanding athlete.

The Children's Home had a school on campus for "problem" kids, but every day I rode the bus to fourth grade at a public school in Tampa. When the other kids from The Home would be in the back of the bus, throwing paper and raising a ruckus, I was well behaved and well dressed. My hair would be brushed, and my clothes would match and be free of holes. I must have been born a fashion queen or something, because I wanted to look like a normal person: clean, well put-together. People would come up to me and say, "I can't believe you're in foster care." The teachers would be especially encouraging and supportive when they found out I wasn't a "normal" child. School was my sanctuary. Often I was one of the top students in the class, and in fifth grade I was voted student body president.

> I wanted to look like a normal person: clean, well put-together.

A lot of foster kids don't want to be adopted because they think it will be just another unsuccessful placement. The whole idea scares them. But I knew that it was the only way I was going to have a permanent home. On group trips at The Children's Home, we'd drive through wealthy neighborhoods and I'd yell out the van window, "Hey, you want a kid? Does anyone want to adopt a kid?"

home at Last

In the fall of 1997, I found out that a couple from Crystal River, Phil and Gay Courter, was interested in adopting me. Before we met I was given a photo album of their home and family, even their pets. They were in their 50s and had two sons, Blake and Joshua, in college. Phil was a documentary filmmaker, and Gay was a writer who had volunteered for years as a child advocate in the court system (that's how she found out about me). They had a beautiful waterfront home with a boat and a pool. I tried not to get too excited. It was kind of like, okay, another placement. We'll see how it goes.

We had lunch. Phil and Gay seemed like a perfectly nice couple, and that November I moved in. There was a strong affection in their house, and I immediately felt welcomed and loved. The house is on the water, and I could watch ospreys pluck fish out of the bay and dive off the dock to swim with manatees. I knew that I would be here forever. Phil and Gay finalized my adoption in July 1998, when I was twelve. I adjusted well to my new life (I'd had a lot of practice adjusting). At Crystal River Middle School I made the honor roll, edited the

Ashley flourished when she went to live with Phil and Gay Courter, making her middle school honor roll and joining the basketball team.

literary magazine, worked on the yearbook and played on the softball and basketball teams. But I never forgot how lucky I was. So many teens in foster care will never find families or have what I have: a place to always call home.

I decided to try to do what I could to improve the system. I narrated a training video that my dad made for the Dave Thomas Foundation for Adoption, an advocacy group started by the founder of Wendy's. In January 1999, I was asked to represent the foundation at a White House ceremony where Hillary Clinton, who has always taken an interest in child welfare, was announcing some new initiatives to support kids in foster care. And I started speaking to groups around the country about my experiences being adopted out of the foster care system. I couldn't forget how the Mosses had treated me and the other kids. I thought the system was so unfair and wrong, to allow people like that to take in and abuse more and more kids. How did they get away with it?

a twist of FATE

Every now and then I'd say to my parents, "Gee, wouldn't it be nice to sue the Mosses for everything they did to me? Is there anything that we can do?" Then early last year I saw the movie *Erin Brockovich* and said to Phil and Gay, why can't we do a class action

Ashley speaking on Capitol Hill to members of the congressional subcommittee on adoption and nearly five hundred participants of the Casey Family Services' National Post-Adoption Services Conference in December 2000.

Ashley's activism on behalf of all kids in the foster care system has garnered her much attention from people as important as former President Bill Clinton.

suit on behalf of the kids in the Moss home? I was just throwing ideas into the air. I never thought it would happen. But I never thought I'd be adopted, either.

About a month later, in May 2000, we got a phone call from a friend who'd heard something on the news about Charles and Marjorie Moss. The next day we read in the paper that they had been arrested and charged with forty counts of felony child abuse. "I want to testify," I said to my parents. "I want to tell what happened to me."

My parents drove me to the police station, where I gave the sheriff my videotaped testimony. I also started giving interviews to the local papers. One reporter found out that the State Department of Children and Families knew about the abuse seven years ago and had allowed the Mosses to adopt the children anyway. As the story of what the Mosses did got out, more kids started coming out of the woodwork. A child rights attorney in Tallahassee filed a class action lawsuit against Governor Jeb Bush and the Florida State Department of Children and Families. Jeremy, who still lives at The Children's Home, is part of that lawsuit, but because I'm out of the system, my parents are suing the state for monetary damages on my behalf. I don't need the money, but Jeremy does. He'll need long-term care to help repair the damage he suffered at the hands of the Mosses. They deserve to pay for this; "I'm sorry" won't cut it.

Two months after the Mosses were arrested, my mom suggested I enter a national essay contest called "How the Harry Potter Books Have Changed My Life." I had read *Harry Potter and the Sorcerer's Stone* in 1999 and was amazed at how

They deserve to pay for this; "I'm sorry" won't cut it.

similar Harry's life was to mine. We were the same age; he too was treated cruelly by a foster family, and Hogwarts Academy reminded me of The Children's Home. I wrote a short essay comparing Harry's life with mine, including descriptions of what the Mosses did to me. On October 2, 2000, I got a phone call telling me I was one of ten winners out of ten thousand entries. I was so excited! The prize was a trip to New York City, breakfast with J. K. Rowling and an appearance on the *Today* show. My essay was even printed in *USA Today*, and Hillary Clinton read part of it on *The Rosie O'Donnell Show*, where they were discussing adoption. Hillary Clinton and I started corresponding, and last December she invited me to a Christmas party. There I was, a kid who seven years ago lived in a blue trailer, shaking hands with the President and First Lady of the United States in the White House.

I believe everything happens for a reason. Even though I've had very bad experiences, those experiences have made me stronger. I want to help improve the foster care system so other kids don't have to suffer like I did. I've talked to children's advocacy groups in several states about my experiences and I've traveled to Washington, D.C., twice to speak at national child-welfare conferences before thousands of people. Somewhere in there I've managed to play varsity basketball, host a local cable show about teens and get my learner's permit. My life's not exactly normal, but it is better than I ever could have imagined. I'm living proof of what I say in my speeches: What kids need are families, not programs.

From babyhood to adulthood, Ashley's life has been difficult. But she's come out on the other side stronger for it, and set on doing what she can to make sure other kids don't have to go through what she did.

Ashley Rhodes-Courter: Escape from Foster Care

Elisa Donovan:

Starving *for* *Success*

ON THE SURFACE, *SABRINA, THE TEENAGE WITCH* STAR ELISA DONOVAN WAS LIVING THE PERFECT HOLLYWOOD LIFE. BUT PRIVATELY, HER BATTLE WITH ANOREXIA NERVOSA WAS EATING AWAY AT HER—LITERALLY.

ELISA DONOVAN
EDITED BY CYNTHIA WANG

'M TWENTY YEARS OLD, AND SO MUCH IS CHANGING IN MY LIFE THESE DAYS.

I was at breakfast recently, talking to someone. For some reason, I was uncomfortable in the conversation, so I went to put something in my mouth. Before I could bite into it, I stopped. I put it down and kept talking. I felt this sense of strength. I can do this! I've decided to restrict my diet and get my life under control.

I have made the big commitment to move from New York to Los Angeles in order to audition for more acting parts. Upon arriving, I go straight to my friend Jennifer's apartment. She's a writer, and she's the one person I know in L.A. She has allowed me to stay with her awhile. When I get to her place, the first thing she says to me is, "Oh, my God! You are so thin!" Hmm. My diet plan must be working, but what is she really saying by pointing out my "thinness"? If anything, I don't think I'm thin enough. In Los Angeles, everyone is so body conscious. There are a lot of women with breast implants, for instance, but I don't want that. I just want to be thin.

I landed a role as Joey Lawrence's girlfriend Tanya on *Blossom*! It's really exciting and terrifying for me because this is my first live sitcom. My weight has dropped significantly since I started watching it at the beginning of the year, so on the set of *Blossom*, I try not to eat anything. One day, I ate half a bagel and I kept thinking about it! Maybe I should have eaten just a quarter of it. I was thinking this all the way until I had to shoot a scene. I heard that if you eat bread or carbohydrates, you will gain weight instantly! I've usually been eating only some grapes. In the morning I eat half a teaspoon of yogurt and then I have grapes at night. Every three to four days I let myself eat a bit of sushi without the rice, like a bit of sashimi. I'm a little hyper now, but this new diet makes me feel like I'm having a spiritual experience or something. I feel like I'm closer to God and more in tune with things, I don't know why.

"I have a journal that I write my dreams in," says Elisa.

I am more than a year into my diet, and people really notice how thin I am. I was out in the sun the other day, sunbathing for I think two hours. After I got up,

I started feeling really dizzy. Jennifer, my roommate, gave me this look and told me, "Maybe you're dizzy because you haven't been eating anything. Get something to eat." Personally, I don't think that's the problem. We go into a restaurant, though. I excuse myself from the table to go to the bathroom, then the strangest thing happens. As I'm going into the rest room, I must have passed out, because I wake up later and I'm on the floor. I pick myself up to go back to the table. As I'm walking toward it, I notice that people are staring at me! Wow, I must look really good.

NOVEMBER 1994:

I'm really excited because I've been cast in what's going to be a great movie! It's called *Clueless*, and I am going to be playing a girl named Amber. One of the costars is Alicia Silverstone! The first day on the set was great because the wardrobe people were really happy to work with me. They tell me they can put almost anything on me! But once again, a strange thing occurred. I was looking in the mirror during one of my fittings when Alicia came up behind me. She looked at me in the mirror, too, and said, "You're going to die soon." I said, "What?" And she said, "You're way too thin." I tell her no, that I do eat a lot of protein. When she leaves, I think what she's told me is great news because I think I'm losing more weight.

FEBRUARY 1995:

I am finishing filming *Clueless* but starting a different, personal project. I finally decided to call up a nutritionist. I had a pretty frightening episode last month when I was hospitalized for passing out. The doctors tried to tell me it was related to my lack of food, but I didn't really think it was a problem. But the more people said things about it, the more I started to think that things aren't normal. I meet with the nutritionist and have no idea what to expect because I still don't consider myself anorexic. I have heard the word, but I don't think it's me at all. For one thing, I think about food all the time and I have always thought that anorexics don't think about food. Besides, I think I'm way too heavy to be an anorexic. But the nutritionist gives me a list of foods, a whole myriad of foods, and I have to check off which ones I think are safe or unsafe, or which ones I like or don't like. I go down the entire list, and the only thing that is safe for me are grapes. As far as what I like or don't like, it occurs to me that I don't know. I don't know anymore! Everything is just bad. So we set up a food plan, something to shoot toward. I will meet with the nutritionist twice a week and she will weigh me for health reasons. She says she needs to know what I am doing, but she will never tell me what the weight is. That's terrifying to me! And I have had a whole series of medical tests. They test your bone tissue for osteoporosis and things like that. I had a certain amount of bone mass loss, so I have to take calcium. I am also starting to see a therapist.

I think about food all the time.

MARCH 1995:

I know there's a problem, but the only thing I can see as a problem is that I can't focus on my work and I can't think about anything else but food. I'm afraid of food, but I still don't think there's anything wrong with my weight. I have a fear of eating too much because if I eat one thing, I think I will keep on eating. I am afraid I won't be able to control it! The only reason to want to be okay, actually, is because I'm afraid to screw up my job. I've been auditioning for five different TV pilots and so far I haven't gotten any of them. One was a sitcom pilot for a girl who is a workout trainer who is manic and crazy. I thought I was perfect for it because I thought I was that girl! When I didn't get the part, I thought it was because I was too fat. I had worn a sleeveless leotard and a skirt to the audition. The way the casting people were looking at me, I thought they thought, "She has no business wearing that." Later, the casting director called my agent, saying I was too skinny. Too skinny? What's the deal? Well, at least that's a good thing—I'm still skinny.

APRIL 1995:

I'm starting to realize how much of my life I have really lost, how many aspects of it. I don't spend time with my friends anymore. I never answer the phone, I never go out. And I don't feel like dating or seeing anyone. All I do is audition, and maybe see some people for coffee. Maybe. My therapist asks me what keeps me so busy then, because I'm always saying that I am. She asks me to break down a typical day when I'm not working,

Elisa Donovan: Starving for Success

what is it that I'm so busy doing. And it's nothing! I work out and think about when I'm going to eat grapes. That's what the day consists of. Wow. Slowly, I start to see that I am losing my creativity. I am losing my thinking mind and I have stopped enjoying things. My nutritionist says that not eating deprives me of the natural energy food provides to fuel the body. Without vitamins, my skin has become sensitive to changes in temperature, and without nutrients, I feel mentally numb sometimes. They want me to start taking hormones but I don't want to because I know that taking hormones will cause me to gain weight.

MAY 1995:

I'm starting to feel weight gain. I can't help but remember what happened in February when I first started eating more foods again. I ate a bagel one day and I started to sweat! I got completely freaked out and I called my nutritionist and I told her, "See? I have this thing, I can't eat carbohydrates, they don't agree with me, it's bad for me." But she said, "Do you understand? You're sweating because your body is working so hard to digest this food! Your sweating is like if you were running." I was, like, whoa! Actually, it isn't even so much that I'm gaining weight as I'm becoming hydrated, but the feeling is so strong and different to me. Now I feel enormous and I'm really, really scared. I decide to stop eating again.

JUNE 1995:

I went to the screening of *Clueless*, which is finally out! The screening was for actors and the press. Somebody said to me, "My God! You're like a bone, a stick." It's what they say to me all the time, so I answered, "Oh, I eat a lot of protein." I didn't think I was lying, but I was. And at the screening, I recall watching the whole movie and seeing Alicia and Stacey and seeing how wonderful the end product was, how funny and silly it was and how beautiful Alicia looked! And I'm thinking, Here I am, sitting here, and I'm cold, and I'm bony, and I'm sitting among all the other actors with probably the

I feel enormous and I'm really, really scared.

Elisa reads to the kids at the Dolphin House: "It makes me happy to make them happy."

smallest part in the movie. I'm thinking, So, this is my success. Yet, in my mind, I'm also thinking, But I'm still the skinniest. I thought I was the better for it, but then I realized it doesn't make a bit of difference! Alicia and I are vastly different body types, but nobody cares. Nobody cares.

JULY 1995:

I'm going to be playing Ginger, Tiffani-Amber Thiessen's best friend, and Jason Priestley's girlfriend, on *Beverly Hills, 90210*. Actually, I had to be in bed with Jason in my first scene on the show! He said, "I know this is weird, but you'll be okay," and he was right. Everyone is so nice on the show. Now I work long days, but it's okay. At first I felt relief and happiness in going back to my old "eating habits." But after the epiphany I had at the *Clueless* premiere, I am trying to resume my food plan. I've eaten lunch with Tiffani-Amber and Jennie Garth, and sometimes with Tori Spelling. I had yogurt and bran cereal because everything is rationed out on the food plan. The other actresses ordered anything from wherever we were eating. They looked at me strangely. It's better sometimes to eat by myself. Once, they asked what I was eating but I didn't want to talk about it. I saw them once, splitting a bag of Jelly Bellys, separating the ones they liked and didn't like, then eating them. I so much want to be normal and to do that! But I just can't. I am so abnormal.

Elisa Donovan: Starving for Success

SEPTEMBER 1995:

I've been going to a therapy group for anorexics and bulimics for almost two months now. Although the members of the group recognized me from the movie, they didn't bring it up. They didn't make me feel less comfortable or less safe in revealing myself, because talking to other anorexics helps me a lot. It helps break the secret because even telling anyone about your food rituals is a big deal. In my case, I had to cut things in a certain way, and different foods couldn't touch each other. Like when I'd eat sushi, I would remove the rice from the fish, but starting at the point where the seaweed and rice were joined together, and then the fish couldn't have any rice touching it because if there were still parts of the rice touching the fish, I couldn't eat it. Or I'd eat egg whites and toast for a meal, and they would bring the food to my table and I would cry. I felt I was eating too much and I felt I was being forced to eat. I would see liquid on the plate, which actually was water, and I would be convinced it was oil, and I can't eat things cooked in oil. So I would keep returning the plate two or three times. Any reason not to eat it! Just telling someone about that was very helpful. Talking to others makes the rituals less unique. What you thought was so special once, now you see others doing the same thing.

DECEMBER 1995:

Beverly Hills, 90210 producer Aaron Spelling is having a huge Christmas party at the Regent Beverly Wilshire Hotel in Beverly Hills. I am terrified to go there! Nervous to be there! I don't really want to wear a dress because I am afraid of exposing my arms, but it is a pretty formal party. So I have decided to wear a dress with a jacket over it, and I can't take the jacket off. I won't take it off, even if it gets uncomfortable. I don't really want people to see my body.

JANUARY 1996:

I've been gaining some weight lately. I don't know how much, but I can tell. It's difficult because I'm afraid people, like the *90210* cast, or even people at various benefits and honorary dinners I go to, will see me and comment, saying, "She's gained weight";

"She's fat"; or "She doesn't look as good as she used to look." I'm afraid people have seen me a certain way and now they will see me differently. With fame, there is a tremendous amount of pressure to continue to perform and be this happy person. People always think, "She's just so happy." Well, the more I eat and recover, the more the layers come off and you see what you're really feeling underneath. I'm so afraid people are going to see this ugliness and anger, these different feelings underneath, and they aren't going to like it! People aren't going to like me because they aren't going to want this person who has things to say and doesn't love everything all the time. But I have to keep recovering. I just have to eat and not think about it and move on.

FEBRUARY 1996:

I still have a specific fear of fittings and wardrobe people. It seemed so easy when I first started, but now they tell me I have "grown up"! It's interesting. Everyone's comment is always, like, "You look great; you look healthy." I think I have to learn how to take these compliments. To them, they see a thin person. They see a thin girl who is not sick. I still think, however, How can they say they see a thin person? The people in wardrobe still think they can put me in anything, but I'm thinking, How can they say that? They must be saying that to make me feel better.

FALL 1996:

I am back with the *Clueless* gang as we shoot the television series based on the movie. Although Alicia is not here, a new actress, Rachel Blanchard, is. She's really nice. I never really speak to Rachel about my eating habits much, but we do speak about body image and what sort of image we are portraying for young people. She doesn't want to present an image that is unattainable. Stacey Dash, though, is still more the person I speak to about it because she knew me from the movie and has been a dear friend ever since. She is an ideal friend of mine! One of the things I love most about her is she's so blatantly honest with me! She and I remember one time the most from filming *Clueless*. She had seen me outside her trailer and I was freezing cold, even though it was bright sun and I was wearing sweatpants. You could see, though, that I had no butt. It just went straight down! One of the actresses said, "God, you are so thin!" I was, like, "No, it's my sweatpants." I caught Stacey's eye and she just looked at me, gave me this look and rolled her eyes. She took me into her trailer later and was, like, "What's your problem? Your body's got to catch up with your head!" And she meant that literally! She keeps me in check. She is a person who will be straight with me. I can talk to her, which helps me a lot.

DECEMBER 1996:

I've gotten a lot of letters from girls who read the *People* article I just did about suffering from anorexia or saw me on *Entertainment Tonight*. Those fans I write back to immediately. There's one girl who is nineteen, who I speak to on the phone a lot. She's from Ohio. She had seen the story and she was really struggling and she wanted to talk to me. As for me, things are getting better. For instance, when I was really starving, I thought I was beautiful and attractive and men loved it. But in reality, they thought I was really skinny and did not find it attractive at all. I didn't realize it at the time. When you don't have nutrients, nothing functions properly. I still don't have my period—haven't had it for a couple of years now—so that affects my hormones. I'm still not fully in touch with my emotions. I don't know what it's like to have a crush anymore! It's so sad because that's one of the most wonderful feelings in the world. And once I started recovering, I was so ashamed of my body. I hated how it looked, hated everything about it. I didn't want to be around men. That was slow, getting to realize that my body is not the most important thing and it's not the only thing men look at or are interested in. Actually, I am dating—Dodd, an art director and designer I met through a mutual friend a few months ago. It's the first relationship that I've started in which I'm beginning to accept myself and be happy about it. Before, I didn't want anyone to touch me, certainly. But we still have difficulties relating to my problems. He's a great guy, but it's very hard.

FEBRUARY 1997:

We finished shooting *Clueless* and soon I'll be starting work on a TV movie. My period has come back to me. I hate it! I hate it because it means that I am healthy. I have to admit to myself, though, that this is better, and normal. From time to time, though, I go back to the way I was. I stop eating for a couple of days or I restrict my eating for a couple of weeks. But because of the knowledge and awareness that I now have, I can't even trick myself anymore. My intention is to pull the reins back and control things again and strive for perfection, but I know now what the reality is. There is no connection between pushing away food and success. There is no connection.

SUMMER 1997:

How crazy is this: I'm shooting the second season of *Clueless* in the mornings, and working on the set of a *Saturday Night Live* movie, *A Night at the*

Elisa's new outlook: "I'm getting more and more comfortable with my body."

Roxbury, in the evenings! Some days I work twenty-three hours a day straight. I knew from the beginning that the old me would've been, like, this is the perfect opportunity to just soar and not eat a thing. Now I realize this is something I have to be adamant about and stringent with myself. I must eat! And I have to eat more than normal because I need to make sure I have all the proper nutrients so I won't get sick, so I can be awake and perform. I have to eat without thinking, no messing with it. Actually, one of the wardrobe assistants on *A Night at the Roxbury*, a comedy in which I play one of the women interested in those dancing guys from *SNL*, is an assistant from the movie *Clueless*. She said, "Look at you! You're so grown up! You were like a little girl when we did the movie and now look!" She literally thought I had been fifteen or something when we did the movie, when I had actually been twenty-three. It was as if I had developed and gone through puberty or something after we did the movie. I was horrified that she could say that! But someone who knew me when she said that told me, "She's complimenting you, don't you see?" I was, like, "Oh, my God!" Now when I see pictures of myself from the movie, I can see I looked skinny, but I never saw that then. Another thing—we had to shoot a fun dancing scene for *Roxbury*. I had so much fun. I can't wait to see it in theaters next spring!

Elisa Donovan: Starving for Success

I've started a great relationship with a sixteen-year-old girl in Illinois. She wrote a very serious letter in which she seemed unwilling to stop or change. She just wanted someone to know because she hadn't told anyone. I immediately wrote back to her. I think she was surprised I wrote back! These letters are great for support because there is still the tendency for me to want to go back to the old way, and here these girls are so young, and I'm hearing them saying the same things that I've said or felt, and it really reminds me of how sad it is.

MARCH 1998:

I went to the premiere of *Scream 2* last week and it was the first time I ever had popcorn at a movie! It felt weird. But it's all part of my life now that I am twenty-five. I read stories to inner-city kids at a charity program called the Dolphin House. It's great because they crawl all over me and like to hear the stories. I'm working on an independent movie in Portland called *Pop*, a film noir comedy. And I'm dating someone new (although I've remained friends with Dodd). He knows me as I am now. It's great to be able to go out to dinner. I love sushi, but now I eat the rice. And I've discovered sushi is really good with the rice! But it's nice to know we can go to other places, too. And that goes for my friends, as well as business lunches, too. But sometimes, I still want to look the way I was, and that's not a good thing. I had thought that people with anorexia were skinny. I'm a big-boned person, not large, but my bone structure is such that when people started telling me I had an eating disorder, I was, like, "What are you talking about? I would rather be that!" But now I realize the body I desired was not physically possible for me to achieve. I wanted my bone structure to change, and that is something, no matter how much I starve myself, I can't change. I have a friend who has a six-year-old daughter. One time I heard her say, "Mommy, I don't want to wear this dress because I'm fat." That made me so sick! What makes her say that? With feminism, girls think they can do anything, which is great. But the pressure, the need to be thin and beautiful aesthetically, is still there.

fast-forward

In 1998, I shared the story of my battle with anorexia with the readers of *Teen People*. I still receive letters from fans who read my story and are struggling with anorexia themselves, and I always answer them right away. I hope it helps them to know that today I feel better than I have felt in my entire life. Last year I joined the cast of *Sabrina, the Teenage Witch* on the WB. It's great to be able to go to wardrobe fittings and feel happy with my body and how I look.

Recently when all of those articles came out about the pressure to be thin in Hollywood, I realized that a lot of actresses I know had literally shrunk. Instead of making me want to be skinny again, seeing them gave me added motivation to stay healthy. Their skin-and-bones look was unattractive and boring to me. This may sound bizarre, but I actually felt fortunate that I'd already survived an eating disorder and put it behind me. The first two years of recovery were the most difficult and full of ups and downs, but I have remained diligent. I still see a therapist. And if I start feeling fat, I ask myself what I'm really upset about: Am I frustrated? Am I stressed out? Am I overtired? Then I deal with the real issue.

The driving force in my recovery has always been that I wanted my life back. I am proud to say that I absolutely have that now.

Today, Elisa looks and feels better than ever.

Jessi Ulmer:

Cancer
Survivor

AFTER CONQUERING A BRAIN TUMOR, A
SHY, SMALL-TOWN GIRL FINDS THE INNER
STRENGTH SHE NEEDS TO CONQUER HIGH
SCHOOL.

JESSI ULMER
AS TOLD TO DANA WHITE

IN JANUARY 1999, I WAS A FRESHMAN AT BELCHERTOWN HIGH, A SCHOOL OF ABOUT 550 KIDS IN THE SMALL TOWN OF BELCHERTOWN, MASSACHUSETTS.

I'd made a few new friends, but I was basically a shy, timid person. Part of the reason for my shyness was that I spent elementary school being called "fat" and "four-eyes." Kids would gang up on me in a big circle and call me names, or make fun of me in class until I blew up. Finally I just shut down and stopped talking.

TEEN PEOPLE: Real Life Diaries

In the sixth grade the teasing got so bad that my mom, Aileen, asked the vice principal at the middle school if I could skip the seventh grade to get away from the kids who were tormenting me. (I also wanted classes that were more challenging.) Eighth grade was less painful, but I was so invisible that a lot of kids thought I'd just moved to Belchertown, even though I'm a third-generation townie. When one girl asked me, "Where did you transfer from?" I answered, "The sixth grade."

Talking to new people was really hard for me. Face-to-face with kids at school—especially boys—I'd sort of blush and search for something to say. I rarely went to parties or school dances. Even at family gatherings, if a relative came up to talk to me I'd say, "Oh, hi," and hide behind my mom. Which is hard, because my mom is smaller than I am.

When I started ninth grade, I was only thirteen. This made me the youngest student at Belchertown High. Still, I was adjusting; I'd gotten good grades (as usual) on my first report card and was helping to start the school's first chorus club. (Other than studying, singing is what I really love to do.) But I was most proud of the fact that finally, for the first time in my life, I'd managed to grow my hair all one length—down to the middle of my back. Life was pretty good.

And then, out of the blue, it wasn't.

Deadly diagnosis

In January, at the beginning of my second semester, I started getting terrible headaches. I managed to go to school, but by February I couldn't keep food down. I'd wake up, throw up and not want to get out of bed. Then my vision got messed up. I couldn't read; the words were shaky and out of focus. This drove me crazy because I was falling behind in my schoolwork. At first my mom wasn't too worried; she thought I just had a bug or needed new glasses. But by the end of

Jessi Ulmer: Cancer Survivor

February, when I was only getting worse, she called my pediatrician. After hearing the symptoms the doctor told her to take me to the hospital immediately for a CAT scan.

"Well, they think there might be a tumor."

On Saturday, February 27, my mom and I drove to the hospital in Palmer, a nearby town, for the test. I'd had a CAT scan before, when my sinuses were acting up, so it wasn't a big deal. My mom wasn't that panicked; we were just getting me checked out. On Monday, the pediatrician called to tell us the test was inconclusive and I needed an MRI, a more complicated test that gives a three-dimensional view of the body. So that afternoon we drove forty minutes to the biggest hospital in the area, Baystate Medical Center, in Springfield. We were both starting to worry that something was definitely wrong.

We got to Baystate at about three in the afternoon. First the radiologist had me lie down on a table in the MRI room. Then he put this helmetlike thing on me and strapped my head to the table to keep it still. Then I was slid up into this big tube. I just had to lie there. It was really claustrophobic and loud in the tube, like a rhythmic thumping that changed in speed and pitch. After thirty-five minutes they took me out and injected a dye into my bloodstream, which would give the radiologist a high-contrast picture of what was going on in my brain. Then I was sent back into the tube for another twenty minutes. The process was boring and freaky at the same time.

Afterward, my mom and I had to wait forever for the results. Finally, at around 6:00, the doctors took my mom into a little dark room. When she came

Jessi working at her father's diner.

back to the waiting room, I knew something was wrong because she was crying.

I said, "Mom, what is it, what's wrong with me? I'm going to be okay. Whatever you tell me, I'm going to be okay."

She said, "Well, they think there might be a tumor."

I asked her if I was going to be admitted. She said they were getting a room ready for me, and the surgery would happen in the next couple of days. The tumor was sitting right on top of my spinal column. The doctors wouldn't know if it was cancerous until they did a biopsy after the operation. But they did know that if it wasn't removed right away, I'd have only a few more months to live.

I just kept telling my mom that I was going to make it. It was strange to be comforting her even though I was the one who was sick. For her sake, I was trying to put a good face on my feelings, but inside I was scared.

under the Knife

We still had to give my dad, Dale, the bad news. At the time my dad was a window salesman who was on the road all the time (now he owns a restaurant), so we couldn't reach him. My mom left a message at his company's main office. He showed up right as we were checking into my hospital room. He was freaking out and crying, "Oh, my God, what are we going to do?" (I may be his oldest daughter, but I'm still his baby.) My mom, who was trying to be calm, said, "We'll take it day by day. We're waiting for the doctors to come." When the doctors came, my dad started yelling at them. I was the optimistic one. "They're going to get it," I said. "I'm going to be okay."

My surgery took place on March 4, 1999. My neurosurgeon, Dr. Kamal Kalia,

"I'm going to be okay."

Jessi Ulmer: Cancer Survivor

cut me open from the base of my neck to the bottom of my cranium. He removed a little trapdoor of bone, carefully cut the tumor out and replaced the bone, fusing it back to the rest of my skull. (Later, when I'd move my head, I could feel the loose bone crunching.) It was a tricky procedure—part of the tumor was growing down into my spinal cord—and it took all day. My mother told me later that while the operation was happening my younger sister, Barbra, who was in sixth grade at the time, congregated in the school counselor's office with some of my middle school friends and cried.

After the operation, the doctors told us the tumor was cancerous. I don't remember my reaction or anyone else's, because I was heavily sedated. I had a malignant tumor called an ependymoma. It was about the size of a walnut and had been growing rapidly. The good news was that the surgeon got the whole thing; they said that with radiation my prognosis was good.

The bad news was that I got pneumonia a few days after the surgery. I was in the Pediatric Intensive Care Unit (PICU) when one of my lungs filled with fluid and collapsed. I had to be wheeled back to the operating room so the doctors could stick a respirator tube down my throat to help me breathe. Back in the recovery room, I woke up, still under sedation, and pulled the tube out. I didn't know what I was doing; all I knew was that there was something in my throat and I wanted it out. The doctors decided to see if I could breathe without the respirator, but I couldn't. I don't like to use the word "die," but I came closest to not making it on March 7. I faintly remember coughing violently and my dad beating on my back to help me breathe, yelling at the doctors to put the tube back in, which they did. I had tubes draining fluid out of my head, and the nurses tied my arms to the sides of my bed to make sure I couldn't pull them out, too. The respirator came out after a few days—it was nice to be able to breathe on my own—but I was tied to my bed for a week.

> # I don't like to use the word "die," but I came closest to not making it on March 7.

MOM
to the Rescue

My mom was my rock. She took a leave from her job delivering flowers to stay with me. She and my dad alternated shifts, sleeping every night on a big easy chair in my room. My mom and I have always been close—I can tell her anything—and this experience made us even closer.

There was nothing to do in the PICU. My face was too swollen for glasses, so watching TV was out. I couldn't talk because of the respirator. And with my hands tied down, that pretty much left my ears for entertainment. My mom brought in a boom box and some CDs so I could have music in my room. My favorite band is No Doubt (I've loved them forever), but I couldn't bear to hear them then because I couldn't sing along. So mom sang along to the radio and read me the many get-well-soon cards I was collecting—anything to take my mind off the situation. Once in a while she would loosen the restraints so I could scratch my nose or write on a notepad the nurses had given me.

But we usually communicated with our hands. My mother had a brother who was deaf, so a long time ago she had taught my sister and me the letters and alphabet in sign language. One day, while still in the PICU, I signed that I wanted to see myself. A nurse brought in a large mirror and held it in front of my face. My mom says that my eyes got really big. I had tubes sticking out all over the place and a respirator down my throat. I looked like a science project. Worst of all, the hair on the top of my head had been shaved off, along with a two-inch-wide strip down the back. I'd been so proud of my long hair. Then the doctors had had to go and do this.

> My mom was my rock.

In early March, I was moved to the adolescent ward. A couple of weeks later, my head started hurting. The doctors did a lumbar puncture—they put a needle in my spine to draw out some spinal fluid—and diagnosed me as having bacterial meningitis. Apparently the incisions had opened up and leaked cerebral spinal fluid, which got infected. Because meningitis is so contagious, I had to be

41

Jessi Ulmer: Cancer Survivor

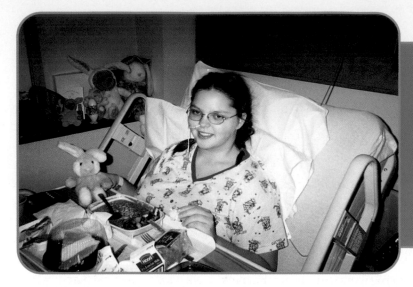

Jessi's first meal in five and a half weeks with Mr. Bunny before radiation treatment started. Jessi received Mr. Bunny when she was born, and he was with her through the entire hospital stay and through every procedure.

quarantined in a separate room for twenty-four hours. It was just me and my mom. Anyone who came into the room had to wear a surgical mask, which made me a little angry. It was as if I had the plague or something.

The doctors didn't want to tell me much because I was only thirteen. I didn't want them sticking needles into me without knowing what the heck they were doing and why, but I couldn't talk even after the respirator was taken out. My mom was my voice. She told the doctors flat out, "Just tell her what's going on. She's an intelligent girl, and she'll understand." After that, they started clueing me in.

Belchertown Steps Up

Originally I was supposed to be in the hospital for two weeks, but because of the complications, that two weeks turned into three, then four. It was scary being in the hospital that long. Sometimes I cried because I was in pain, or because I just didn't want to be in that bed anymore. Other times I was just scared. I had cancer and all this stuff was happening and I didn't know exactly what was going on. Why did I have to go through this? I'd always been a good person. If someone at school was in trouble or needed help with their homework, I wouldn't look the other way. It didn't seem fair. When I got really down, my mom would sit on the edge of my bed and tell me we'd get through it, I just had to be patient.

Fortunately, I had lots of visitors and gifts. Everyone at my high school, people at the church we used to go to, my mom's coworkers and random people in Belchertown sent me stuff. Even my fourth-grade teacher came and brought me a stuffed bunny. Looking back, the most amazing thing was how the people of Belchertown rallied around me. I had churches all over western Massachusetts praying for me, and everyone at school signed this big poster. The Belchertown Teen Center did a can drive. The high school held a Jessi Ulmer dance, and my mom's coworkers sold green and white carnations on Saint Patrick's Day and gave all the money to me. Our insurance covered my hospital bills, but the money helped pay for other costs. I needed a new wardrobe—because I lost forty pounds in the hospital— and millions of bandannas to cover my funky haircut.

Finally, on April 16, six weeks after I was admitted, I walked out of Baystate on shaky legs with my parents and sister. When we got home I kissed my dog and my three cats. Home. I was home. Then I walked through my bedroom door and stopped in my tracks. My queen-sized bed was piled high with all the presents I'd received. I was amazed—I never knew there were that many people in Belchertown who cared about me.

Jessi (right) with her little sister after two and a half days at Belchertown's annual fair—and more than a year after Jessi's surgery.

Jessi Ulmer: Cancer Survivor

Jessi doing her second favorite thing besides singing . . . reading!

the Visible Girl

Every weekday for five weeks my mom drove me to Baystate for radiation treatments to kill any stray cancer cells. This big machine would blast radiation into each side of my head for about five minutes. I didn't really feel any physical effects except all the hair on the back of my head fell out underneath (that was a really great look), and the steroid I was on made me gain all the weight back, though I managed to lose most of it all again.

I spent that summer recuperating, taking naps and making up my schoolwork with a tutor. My muscles were weak and I got tired easily. When I went back to school in the fall of 1999 for my sophomore year, I was a little nervous about staying on my feet for six and a half

Jessi with her fellow singers during a recent chorus rehearsal. Left to right: Kaitlen, Jessi, and one of Jessi's closest friends, Andrea.

hours. But I did it! My teachers were really understanding, but my friends seemed a little scared of me. I'd cough and they'd go, "Are you okay?" Some of my friends didn't know how to act around me. They thought I was more delicate. I was, like, I'm a big girl, I can take care of myself. I'm not going to break.

More than two years later I'm cancer free. I have to go back for regular checkups, but I don't think my cancer will come back. I know it won't.

I'll never be quite the same. Now I have a plastic tube called a shunt that drains excess brain fluid from my skull to my stomach. And I still have a bald spot on either side of my head where the radiation went in. The rest of my hair has grown back thin and sparse, though at least it's long enough to pull into a ponytail.

I can't say that having cancer has changed my life, but it has changed my outlook on life. I live more for today. I can't live for tomorrow because tomorrow might not be there. And having cancer has made me stronger. Now I don't worry as much about what other people think. I just walk right up and say hi. I have more friends than I've had my entire life, more than all of my old friends combined. I even got up the nerve

to ask a guy to the junior prom—and he said yes! My mom made my dress, and it's so beautiful: a floor-length off-the-shoulder gown with an empire waist. It's ivory and gold, and modeled after the dress Drew Barrymore wears at the end of the movie *Ever After*. I'm going for the Cinderella theme this year. Now all I need is my prince.

Most of all, I refuse to be invisible. High school is not the easiest place to be, but neither is a hospital bed for six weeks. Going through what I did makes me realize that stuff like cliques and clothes don't really matter. Being popular doesn't make you any more alive.

After six hours of school and six hours of work, Jessi models the new tiara her mother made for her junior prom.

Tyrese:

Making *It*

TYRESE SHARES HOW HE WENT FROM
WATTS, ONE OF LOS ANGELES'S
ROUGHEST NEIGHBORHOODS, TO
BECOME A GUESS? MODEL AND
SINGING SENSATION.

TYRESE GIBSON
AS TOLD TO LINDA FRIEDMAN

I VISIT INNER-CITY SCHOOLS A LOT, AND I ALWAYS TELL THE KIDS I MEET THAT IF I CAN MAKE IT, THEY CAN MAKE IT.

For some reason, kids have a hard time believing that a star like me ever had to struggle. They see me on television wearing designer gear and hanging out with superstars, and they assume I've always lived this glamorous Hollywood life. But I was never the kid who came to school wearing up-to-the-minute brand names. In fact, I was lucky to make it to first period at all because most days I didn't even have a quarter for the bus.

TEEN PEOPLE: Real Life Diaries

I was born and raised in Watts, a tough neighborhood in the notorious South Central section of Los Angeles. I'm the youngest of four siblings. My dad was around some of the time while I was growing up, but it was my mom who raised and supported us by working three different restaurant jobs at once. She definitely had her hands full. I was the kid who always wanted to be the center of attention. And I did whatever it took (goofing off, telling jokes, getting in trouble) to get that attention. When I was seven years old, I got kicked out of public school because I was hyperactive. I had to go to an alternative school for kids with behavioral problems all the way through the eighth grade.

I may have had trouble playing by the rules at school, but I figured out the laws of my neighborhood really fast. My survival depended on it. When you live in the hood, each set of streets has its own set of rules. Once you figure them out, it makes your life a whole lot easier—and a whole lot safer. To stay out of trouble, it was imperative to know where to go and where not to go, what to say and what not to say, and even what to wear and what not to wear.

I also tried to be involved in as many positive activities as I could. I played sports and started singing in local talent shows when I was fourteen. These things saved me from getting attacked by any of the local gangs. If a group of guys was trying to mess with me, one of them would be, like, "Leave him alone, homey. He plays football. He's the quarterback. We need him." Or another would say, "He's the one who's always singing at the park. Leave him be."

Don't get me wrong. I still had to watch my back. I'm going to let you in on my former reality: Red is my favorite color, and I wear red almost every day. When I was in elementary school, I drew and painted

> I was the kid who always wanted to be the center of attention. And I did whatever it took (goofing off, telling jokes, getting in trouble) to get that attention.

> **I'm not saying I never did any bad things. But I stayed away from the serious trouble.**

everything red. But I grew up in Crip hoods, where they wear blue and don't get along with the Bloods, who wear red. So I couldn't express myself by wearing red. To this day, I'm selective about where I wear my favorite color. Now I live in another Los Angeles suburb, but when I go back to Watts, you won't catch me wearing my favorite big old red sweater.

Fortunately, I was smart enough to stay away from the gangs while I was growing up, though I saw enough that I didn't have to do any research for my role as a gangster in the John Singleton movie *Baby Boy*. I'm not saying I never did any bad things. But I stayed away from the serious trouble. I was never in any kind of gang fight or gang war. I managed to avoid most of the stereotypical troubles that trip up a lot of young black males in South Central Los Angeles. I'm pretty proud to be able to say that at twenty-two, being born and raised in Watts, I've never been to jail. That may not sound like much, but trust me, it's a real accomplishment.

The one thing that helped me survive—and ultimately get out of—Watts was that I always had a knack for making the best of a bad situation. And a bad situation was exactly what I was in when I got kicked out of elementary school. At my new school, some of the adults couldn't deal with me—I was too hyper. They would verbally abuse me. Worse yet, I was led to believe that if I ever went back to a normal school, I wouldn't be able to handle it. So when I left that school after eighth grade and enrolled at Locke, a local high school that happened to have a widely respected music department, I was determined to prove them wrong and turn my life around. I flipped a negative situation into a positive one by using it as a motivating force, and I became a straight-A student.

My favorite subject was music. And my music teacher, Mr. Reggie Andrews, became one of my

> **I flipped a negative situation into a positive one by using it as a motivating force, and I became a straight-A student.**

biggest role models. In all my years at school, Mr. Andrews was the first person who saw my potential and encouraged me. After he helped me discover my passion for singing and music, there was no stopping me. During lunch, I learned piano and how to read music. At Locke High School, I was voted most talented.

But my goal was to one day put out my own album. So I watched Black Entertainment Television (BET) and I wrote down the names of the record labels that all the artists were signed to. Then I called information, got the record companies' phone numbers, and called them up. They all told me the same old thing: Send a tape in and we'll see what we can do. But when I called Priority Records, Gayle Atkins, who did promotions for them, was sitting in for the receptionist, who had taken a bathroom break. That's what I call lucky timing. Gayle and I hit it off on the phone, and after she heard my material, she became my manager.

My sophomore year of high school, I got an even bigger lucky break. Mr. Andrews told me that a casting director was looking for a local black male between the ages of sixteen and eighteen to sing in a national Coke ad campaign. I had two days to find a ride to the audition, but when the big day came I still didn't have one. Mr. Andrews offered to drive me after he closed down the music department. But by then rush hour traffic had started, and we arrived at the audition two and a half hours late. The casting lady had already packed up her equipment. The only reason she wasn't out the door was because her ride was stuck in traffic, too. I asked her if I could still try out, but she said no and told me I should learn to get to my auditions on time. I begged her until she finally let me sing. I ended up getting the part, and the rest, as they say, is history.

> I begged her until she finally let me sing. I ended up getting the part, and the rest, as they say, is history.

The commercial, in which I sang "Always Coca-Cola" on a bus, was so popular that it got me jobs hosting *MTV Jams* and doing ads for Tommy Hilfiger. More important, it sparked a record company bidding war. I signed with RCA and soon

Tyrese performs with Jermaine Dupri and Da Brat. Music was his ticket out of Watts, one of L.A.'s toughest neighborhoods.

put out my self-titled debut album that went platinum. My second album, *2000 Watts*, was released last spring.

After the commercial came out, I also became the Coca-Cola youth spokesperson. For three years, I visited high schools and tried to inspire kids by talking about the challenges I faced in my childhood and my community. I got a lot of satisfaction out of it. I've always preferred giving to receiving. I have to give my mom credit for that. Even when she had nothing, she wanted to pay everyone else's bills. When I started being successful, I could have been, like, "I've got mine. I'm gonna keep on getting more and to hell with everybody else." But like music, inspiring others is a passion of mine. I feel like God is using me. If I were to die today, at least I'd know I've given back and made a difference in a lot of people's lives.

I've always preferred giving to receiving. I have to give my mom credit for that.

What I've done so far is just the beginning. After giving my time and energy to support other causes, I decided to create my own charitable organization. Recently some friends from the old neighborhood and I set up the 2000 Watts Foundation to better the lives of the kids in Watts. We're going to build the first boys and girls' youth center in the area, and we'll hire local teachers (the kids will be able to send letters recommending their favorites) to run the programs there. We're also going to refurbish the baseball diamond and soccer field and rebuild the stage at Ted Watkins park, where I did my first talent show when I was fourteen.

Last September, we staged a big fund-raiser, the "First Annual Watts Day." Kobe Bryant, Brandy and Da Brat, along with a bunch of other celebrities, showed up to lend their support. We had rides and arcade games and a talent showcase for the kids. And we raised a lot of money to add to the $100,000 that Oprah Winfrey had already generously donated.

I want to put a map in the boys and girls' youth center

If out of fifty kids I'm able to inspire and change twenty, I'll feel like I'm doing my job.

He may be a big star, but Tyrese will never forget where he comes from.

we're going to build. If a child is able to exceed the education goals we help him set, he'll be able to walk up to the map and point to where he wants to go in the world, and we'll get him there with the help of an airline sponsor. I want each child who comes to the center to have a big brother and a big sister to take him or her places within Watts and then within other parts of California and even the United States and abroad.

"Always remember that if you give from your heart, you can do no wrong."

I may not be able to change all the children and change their state of mind to see the bigger picture. But if out of fifty kids I'm able to inspire and change twenty, I'll feel like I'm doing my job. Those twenty kids will realize that the world consists of more than Watts. And then they might choose to make the best of a challenging situation. That's when I'll sleep even easier at night. That's when I'll feel like I've done God's work. But what I want everyone who's reading this to know is that I'm following my heart. This is how I want to give back. If you want to give back, too, figure out what cause excites you. And always remember that if you give from your heart, you can do no wrong.

Laura Heldt:
i drove
drunk
and killed someone

A WEEK AFTER GRADUATING FROM HIGH SCHOOL, LAURA HELDT WAS ON TOP OF THE WORLD. THEN SHE CAUSED A DEATH WHILE DRIVING DRUNK. HERE, SHE TALKS FROM PRISON ABOUT HER DEADLY MISTAKE.

LAURA HELDT
AS TOLD TO DAVID OLIVER RELIN

UNTIL THE WEEK AFTER I GRADUATED FROM HIGH SCHOOL, WHEN I WAS EIGHTEEN, I HAD WHAT A LOT OF PEOPLE WOULD CALL A PERFECT LIFE.

My parents used to call me "Little Miss Popular" because my phone was always ringing and I was always surrounded by friends. My family was well-off. I had just graduated from Xavier, a prestigious private school in Phoenix, and I'd been accepted to Arizona State University, where I planned to major in dance, which had been my life since I was four. Ballet, tap, jazz, everything.

I was looking forward to the summer because I had graduation trips planned with my friends to Mexico and San Diego. Everything was going so well. Then one night, a week after graduation, I threw it all away.

There was a big keg party planned that night, so I met up with a bunch of girls for a pre-party, where we made a cooler of "jungle juice"—different kinds of hard alcohol mixed with fruit juice. Then five of us left in my Bronco and drove to pick up four guys. My friend Angela was driving my car, because she was the designated driver. I had a sports bottle full of jungle juice and drank it as we drove.

I know now that our concepts about drinking were twisted and naive. I partied with my friends most weekends. Sometimes we would drink until we were belligerently drunk, and even designated drivers would have a couple of drinks. It wasn't any social disgrace. Drinking was considered cool, not dangerous.

When we got to the party, it was huge—some kid whose parents were away had kegs in his backyard. Soon Angela asked if it was cool if she left with her boyfriend. I said that was fine and I'd stop drinking so I could drive. But the police broke up the party about half an hour later and we were in a hurry to leave, so I drove.

I dropped people off until it was just my friend Erin and me in the car. I remember what happened next vividly, completely. I can put myself in that seat again and know exactly what song was playing: Notorious B.I.G.'s "Hypnotize." I'll never forget how loud it was blaring. I paused at a stop sign, not really stopping, just slowing down—and I never saw the car I pulled out in front of. It was a Jeep Wrangler and it slammed into my side of the Bronco.

I can still feel the Bronco rolling over, taste the blood in my mouth and feel my body being tossed around. We rolled and landed on the passenger side. I had my seat belt on, but the crash shot me up through the seat belt and I landed on Erin.

shock, then Breakdown

I banged up my face and had a bloody nose, and Erin banged up her leg, but that was it. I was kicking the stereo because the song would not shut up. We crawled out through the

Stephanie Michelle Jensen, 17 of Glendale, a student at Greenwa High School, die June 2, 1997. Sh was born in U land, Calif., an was in the dram club. Survivors i clude her parent: even and Debbie; sister, Holly Jamiso d brothers, Calvin and Tyler. Service :30 a.m. Saturday, Northwest Comm y Church, 16615 N. 43rd Ave., Pho , with visitation from 9:30 t :30 a.m. Contributions: Greenway Th r Department Stephanie Jensen Sch rship Fund, 3930 W. Greenway Roa

Keep me as the apple of your eye; hide me in the shadow of your wings...

back of the car. Police and ambulances and all kinds of witnesses were there right away. We asked how the people in the other car were, but the police didn't tell us anything.

They checked my blood-alcohol level when I got to the hospital about an hour later. Even by then, it was still .14 percent, nearly one and a half times the legal limit. I spent the night in the hospital, but I was fine. In the morning, when they rolled me out in a wheelchair, there was a police officer waiting. He told my parents he had to arrest me for aggravated assault. As soon as I stood up from that wheelchair, I was cuffed, put in the officer's car and driven to the police station.

I sat in a holding cell with twenty other women fresh off the streets, prostitutes and all kinds of people I'd never had any contact with in my life. I was pretty scared. One of the prostitutes said, "Why are they worried about us? We're not hurting anyone. They should worry about the drunk drivers." I'll never forget that. That made me realize that the trouble I was in was really serious. I had seventeen hours to think about it until my father was able to get me out on bail.

One of the passengers in the other car was named Stephanie Jensen. She was my age. She hit her head during the accident and never regained consciousness. They finally gave up and took her off life support two days later. When I found out she died, it was just like all-at-once shock. That's when I really broke down and fell apart.

I was home alone with my mom that day. We spent the whole day lying in bed, crying. She just held me. I don't think she knew what to say. I couldn't believe how I went from having everything to feeling like I had nothing. I'd taken away a life. I was drowning in grief and guilt.

After the accident, it was seven months until I was sentenced. It was just this haze of pure hell. I tried to start college, but I barely went to class. I was in the psychiatrist's office every day. I attempted suicide. I took a bunch of all the pills I could find, but my boyfriend at the time made me throw them up. I would cut myself really bad. I didn't even know what I was doing. I cut my arms, my face, my stomach. I used razors, glass, anything. I think I wanted the outside of me to be ugly and hurt just like the inside.

> I can still feel the Bronco rolling over, taste the blood in my mouth and feel my body being tossed around.

I never spoke to Stephanie's family. I learned from the newspaper that she had been into theater and drama and that she'd had a lot of friends. She sounded like me. She had red hair—I used to dye mine auburn. From what I know of her, we could have been friends. Completely. A lot of her friends came to my sentencing, and they looked just like mine. Stephanie died on the day she was supposed to graduate from high school. Her friends held a seat for her at the ceremony, just in case.

There was no trial. I just pleaded guilty. My attorney had explained that Arizona had mandatory sentencing laws for anyone eighteen and over, and that I would do time. When the judge said I was going to prison for four years, there was a lot of noise in the courtroom, and some cheering. There was a lot of hate in the room. That's understandable. If someone had killed someone I cared about, I'd be angry, too. I don't consider myself a victim whatsoever.

After I hugged my family and friends good-bye, I was taken to Perryville, a maximum security prison outside Phoenix. It was like nothing I'd ever experienced: being locked in a small cell with other people, feeling dirty all the time, using the bathroom in front of others, people stealing from you and messing with you and getting in your face all the time. You feel really low. You always feel insecure and alone. I thought about my friends off at college having fun. I just kept thinking, What have I done to my life?

Laura Heldt: I Drove Drunk and Killed Someone

TAKING Responsibility

I kept in touch with a lot of my friends. But it made me crazy that what happened to me didn't change their behavior. I learned that one friend was arrested for DUI. An ex-boyfriend sent me photos of all of us partying and wrote, Remember the good times? Those "good times," that underage drinking, was what got me in trouble. It was like a slap in the face—like, hello, I'm here because someone died! I mean, how dare they keep doing that, having seen the consequences?

When I first realized I was going to jail, I thought my whole life was over. Now that I have a little over a year to go here, I'm more positive. I work as a teacher's aide, helping women earn their GEDs, and I've taken self-help and college courses here. But that doesn't mean prison is bearable. I miss home, I miss what matters. Not material things, but my parents, my two sisters, my close friends—and my freedom. Time here goes very slowly.

After I'm released, I'm planning to go back to Arizona State and study dance. I want to look for an apartment close enough to the university so that I don't have to drive. My driver's license has been revoked. I can get it back, but I don't even want to think about getting behind the wheel of a car again. I'm also considering counseling youths. With what I've been through, I think I could make a difference. I've written letters about my experience that my mom and dad have read to teenagers at high schools and churches.

If I learned anything from all of this it's that people need to take responsibility for their actions and not drink and drive because their friends do it. I thought I was a pretty big badass in high school, and look what happened to me. You think nothing bad is ever going to

"Getting shopped" at Perryville, picking up supplies like snacks and toiletries from the prison store. "I don't consider myself a victim whatsoever," Laura says. "I ended Stephanie's life. . . . Because I didn't just stop and think. There's nothing I can ever do to make up for it."

happen to you, but it just might. Whether you're behind the wheel or you're in the car with someone who's drinking and driving, you might die. Or you might be responsible for paralyzing or killing someone else. And believe me, that's a responsibility you don't want to have.

I ended Stephanie's life. I took everything away from her because I was stupid. Because I didn't just stop and think. There's nothing I can ever do to make up for it. My only hope is that my story stops a few of you from making the same mistake.

fast-forward

Four years after her high school graduation, Laura Heldt, twenty-two, is about to celebrate an even more important milestone. On June 12, 2001, she will be released from the Arizona State Penitentiary. During her time behind bars, Laura has kept her spirits up by keeping in touch with her closest friends. She was even listed as an honorary bridesmaid on the program of one of her classmate's weddings. And last fall, she had a bittersweet taste of her upcoming freedom when she was granted a one-day release to attend her grandfather's funeral.

Laura, who was sentenced to prison after killing eighteen-year-old Stephanie Jensen in a drunk-driving accident, is determined to produce something positive from her devastating experience. A gifted dancer since childhood, Laura plans to re-enter Arizona State University, where she enrolled just before her prison term began, and study dance therapy.

Laura in the cell she shares with another inmate at Perryville Prison, outside Phoenix.

Laura says her time in prison has taught her that low-income kids often get into trouble because they are raised with low self-esteem. By combining her passion for dance and the compassion prison has taught her, Laura hopes one day to work providing support and self-esteem to disadvantaged children.

Laura Heldt: I Drove Drunk and Killed Someone

Anthony Colin:

Survivor's Song

ANTHONY, SEVENTEEN, HAS ALWAYS BEEN PROUD TO BE
GAY. TWO YEARS AGO, HIS PRIDE WAS PUT TO THE TEST
WHEN HE TRIED TO START A GAY/STRAIGHT ALLIANCE AT HIS
HIGH SCHOOL IN ORANGE, CALIFORNIA. LITTLE DID HE
KNOW HE WAS IN FOR THE FIGHT OF HIS LIFE.

ANTHONY COLIN
AS TOLD TO DANA WHITE

WHEN I WAS ELEVEN, I TOLD A FRIEND THAT I LIKED BOYS. BUT MY FRIEND HAD A BIG MOUTH, AND SOON THE WHOLE SCHOOL KNEW.

From that point on, there was not a day when I wasn't teased, harassed or threatened because of my sexual preference. I'd been teased since kindergarten for being feminine—I had long hair and a really high voice—but now it got worse. I was called fag, homo, queer—all the horrible names you can think of that are derogatory terms for a homosexual teenager. Still, I wasn't mad at my friend for outing me; it was going to come out sooner or later. And looking back, it was sort of a good thing because it helped me develop the survival skills I'd need later on in my life.

Coming OUT

It took me two years to get up the courage to tell my parents. I told my mom, Jessie, first. We were sitting at the kitchen table at our house in Orange, California, when suddenly I blurted out, "Mom, I think I'm gay." She just looked at me for a second and then burst into tears. Her main concern was that she'd never be a grandmother. I have four sisters (I happen to be the queen of the family), but as the only boy, I was the family legacy, the family name. I was very close to my mother, but we went through a weird, awkward phase as she tried to cope with the news. The best part was that I didn't have to suffer in silence at school anymore. My mom was always at the school fighting for me. Not because I was her gay son, but just because I was her son.

Four months later, we told my dad, Robert. He had always pushed me to play football like he had, and would talk about the day I'd marry a woman and have children. I knew deep down that I couldn't fulfill his masculine expectations, so I withdrew from him. I had a feeling he was going to take my news badly, and he did. My mom and I told him together. (Actually, she told him and I agreed.) First, he was very quiet. Then he said I was choosing to be gay, and that I'd done it to humiliate the family name and him. For a long time he wouldn't speak to me or look at me or even use the word "gay." He'd say, "My son's not 'that way.'" His reaction hurt. Even though we didn't get along all the time, he was still my father and I loved him.

Orange County, California, is one of the most conservative counties in the United States, but my parents are not intolerant people. My dad, an architect, and my mom, a ceramicist, raised my sisters and me to love everybody, regardless of skin color or religion. It just so happened that homosexuality was never brought up at home because neither of my parents knew anyone who was gay. Like many Latino families, we come from a very strong Catholic background where even whispers of homosexuality can make people uneasy. Children from those families who come out are often kicked out of the house or mistreated by their relatives. So in a way, I was lucky.

> "Mom, I think I'm gay."

Anthony Colin: Survivor's Song

An Easy TARGET

In junior high, kids who had attended elementary school with me spread the word that I was gay. I never denied who I was. If somebody came up to me and asked if I was gay, I'd say, "Yes, I am." I displayed a rainbow pin proudly on my backpack.

Soon the harassment turned physical. One day, a couple of guys shoved me into the bathroom, pushed me into a stall and locked me in the bathroom with the lights out. I couldn't get out for an hour. Another time, I was standing in the lunch line when some rocks and pizza came flying at my head. Other Latino students would poke fun at me and push me around. And of course the names continued.

As time went on, I became more and more withdrawn and depressed. My grades and social life suffered. I would never go out with my friends or to club meetings. I always wore dark clothing, and people called me Goth boy (which was better than "sissy," I guess). I couldn't date like everybody else. My friends, who were straight, couldn't relate to me. Ironically, I was the shoulder everyone else cried on because I'd already experienced so much. Someone was having problems with being teased? I'd been there. Having problems with their parents? I'd done that, too. I had no one to depend on except myself.

> The only thing that kept me going to school was my sixth-period choir class.

The only thing that kept me going to school was my sixth-period choir class. Singing was my outlet, the thing I loved the most. I channeled all my pain and frustration into my voice so that when I sang, you knew what I was feeling. My choir teacher asked a few of the students, including me, to sing "The Star-Spangled Banner" at our middle school's volleyball and soccer games. My mom, who was my first music teacher, always told me that the national anthem is not an easy song to sing, and she was right. The words about freedom and justice are beautiful, but I knew they weren't real, at least not for me. But I put my heart into it, hoping that one day that song would come true.

In Memory
of Matthew

In 1998, I started at El Modena High School, just a block from my house. It was not an improvement. I was verbally harassed, spat on and shoved down some stairs from behind. The locker room scene was so intimidating—guys wanted to prove how "masculine" they were by making fun of a gay person—that I was excused from taking PE and allowed to use the faculty bathroom. In my first two years I filed several harassment complaints with school officials, but it didn't do any good.

My freshman year of high school I heard the horrifying news of Matthew Shepard's murder in Wyoming. As someone who had never tried to hide my homosexuality, I'd always felt like an outcast in Orange County. But suddenly I was afraid to walk down the street for fear that I might be the next person killed for being gay. Eventually that fear turned to anger, and the anger to action. I wanted to do something to stop homophobia and to provide a safe haven for other teens like me. That's when I got the idea to start a club at El Modena that would promote understanding and acceptance of all students regardless of race, religion or sexual orientation.

On September 8, 1999, the first week of my sophomore year, I requested an application to start my club. Orange County is home to several conservative religious groups, and I warned my mom that some faculty members might have a problem with the idea. She told me not to worry, she'd take care of it. We had no idea what was coming.

The request had to be approved by the principal. She kept putting me off, and in October she refused to let me have a table at Club Rush, when students find out about new clubs. I was baffled and dumbfounded. The school had clubs for Christian, African-American and Asian teens, among others. Why not gay teens? I took a petition around school and got fifty signatures from students who wanted to join and even more from kids who supported the idea. Then I found out that officials of the Orange Unified School District were going to have a closed-door session about my club. This shocked me—the school district never had to approve clubs.

The Orange County Register somehow found out and ran a short article about the

Anthony Colin: Survivor's Song

meeting. The next day a friend and I were walking to school when a reporter approached us and asked, totally by coincidence, if we were aware of a student on campus who wanted to start a "gay student" club. My friend said, "Yeah, you're looking at him!" After that, my name was printed in every article about the club. Pretty soon it seemed as if the whole county knew who Anthony Colin was.

Law and Disorder

On the night of November 9, the school board held an open forum about the pros and cons of starting what they called a Gay/Straight Alliance (GSA) at El Modena. Hundreds of people packed the room wanting to voice their opinions. Parents and community and religious leaders stood up and said the school board shouldn't allow it because we wanted to talk about having sex. Worse, some people argued that a GSA would turn all the students gay, and that I was going to infect them with AIDS because all gay people have AIDS. The hearing went on for hours, and it was the most gruesome event I've ever witnessed. Like my mom, I'm a small person with a big voice, and I got up to defend the GSA. But it was clear that nothing I could say would change their minds.

The board kept postponing its decision about whether to allow the GSA. On November 23, I started holding unofficial club meetings on the sidewalk across the street from school. The next day, my lawyers from the Lambda Legal Defense and Education Fund, People for the American Way Foundation and a private firm named Irell & Manella filed a lawsuit against the Orange Unified School District. (They filed it on behalf of myself and another GSA advocate, who later dropped out of the suit.) Basically, the suit claimed that the school district was denying us our rights under the 1984 Equal Access Act, which prohibits a school from discriminating against a student club because of its political, philosophical or religious viewpoints.

Finally, on December 7, the school board held another public meeting. This one was even more crowded, as reporters, supporters and protesters carrying signs that said things like "Grades, not AIDS" crammed into the room. I was nervous and anxious, but

"I didn't choose to be an activist; I was born a fighter, just as I was born a homosexual," Anthony says. His greatest supporter since his battle began has been his mom, Jessie.

defiant. No way was I going to be afraid of people who tried to bring me down for who I was. The seven-member school board wanted me to change the club's name to "tolerance group" and restrict what we could talk about, but I refused. Finally, they voted unanimously to ban the GSA from El Modena. The tension in that room was so great that after the decision, as I was making my way outside, an old man smacked me on the head.

The following weeks were really crazy. I was juggling school with conference calls with my lawyers and interviews with reporters. And I was getting a lot of mail, good and bad, but the hate mail threatening to kill me was frightening. One day, I found a letter in my locker that said, "Get the hell out of El Modena." It's no secret where I live, and it was scary not knowing who was going to show up at my door, leave a threatening message on my answering machine or be waiting for me down the street. I made the one-block walk to school accompanied by friends and family. Every day I had to run a gauntlet of protesters—many of them from out of state—who picketed outside the school every day. They called me a subhuman species, a demon, and told me I belonged in hell. It was so surreal to realize that there were people who didn't know me—who didn't even live in California— yet who hated me so much.

By this time, the controversy was affecting my entire family. As always, my mother was right there the whole time fighting with me, letting everyone know that she was backing her son. My dad was coping with it, and he defended me to the newspapers. My two older sisters,

> They called me a subhuman species, a demon, and told me I belonged in hell.

71

Raquel and Regina, were my bodyguards, walking me to board meetings and even to the bathroom. I tried to keep my younger sister, Rusti, as far away from it as I could. She wanted to be cool with her crowd, and it didn't help that she had a gay brother who was practically the most notorious person in Orange County.

JUSTICE at Last

On Monday, January 24, 2000, while everyone else was studying for finals, I was testifying before a judge in a Santa Ana courtroom. My lawyers wanted the federal courts to overrule the school board and let the GSA meet while our case proceeded. On February 4, the judge ruled in our favor. I was at school at the time and didn't know about the ruling until I saw my mother running down the street, clutching a big bunch of rainbow-patterned balloons that bounced in the air behind her. We hugged and cried ecstatically. Her gesture was so touching and reassuring; it let me know that we'd really done it.

The Monday after the judge's decision, students arrived at school to find that someone had plastered the place with flyers that showed two men embracing and the words "Come to El Modena, don't be shy. You're either gay or you're bi." Rival schools had nicknamed us "HomoDena," and obnoxious antigay graffiti was often scrawled everywhere. Many students were furious at me, especially the jocks who played contact sports like water polo and had to take teasing from other teams. When I walked down the halls I could feel the hostility radiating in my direction.

> When I walked down the halls I could feel the hostility radiating in my direction.

Two days later, the first on-campus meeting of the Gay/Straight Alliance was held at El Modena. It was the weirdest day in the history of the school. Protesters from as far away as Utah had thronged just off school grounds, and what seemed like the entire student population was gathered outside the door of the meeting room, booing and jeering at the seventy students (most of them straight) who dared to attend. I had been expecting only fifty.

Oh, my God, I thought as I looked around. It was a big, big day. The meeting lasted about half an hour. We elected club officials, ate cookies and talked about the club mission statement.

When the meeting was over, all hell broke loose. We had to wait twenty minutes for security guards to arrive and escort us through the angry crowd yelling "queer" and "fag" at us. As I was crossing the street I got into a shouting match with a protester from Utah. When my sister Sara tried to pull me away, the protester bonked me on the head with her sign! Sara grabbed the sign and threw it into the crowd. Finally the cops showed up to clear the area.

Loud and PROUD

The hearings and protests continued through the spring. I was exhausted from fighting. Eventually the protesters got tired, too, and the number of people outside the school dwindled. In early September, a year after the whole drama had started, the school district board and my lawyers settled the case, and the GSA was cleared to be an official club on El Modena's campus forever. Choking back tears, I thanked the board members for settling and said I respected them for standing up for what they believed in, just as I had. Outside, I collapsed into my mother's arms and cried. It was a hard battle, but we won. We won.

I didn't choose to be an activist; I was born a fighter, just as I was born a homosexual. My father, who's seen how much I've suffered by standing up for who I am, understands that now. In the spring of 2000, Amnesty International gave me an Enduring Spirit Award for my efforts, and he went with me to the ceremony. And last August, when I was named the 2000 Man of the Year at the Orange County Lesbian and Gay Pride Festival, I dedicated the award to my father, who has come so far.

El Modena has come far, too. The students are totally cool with the GSA; most of them don't even realize it's there. I still speak out for gay youth and give motivational speeches, but I'd love to pursue my dream of being an entertainer. These days I do most of my performing at a karaoke bar across the street from Disneyland, but no matter what the song is, I sing it from the heart, just as my mom taught me to.

73

Anthony Colin: Survivor's Song

Andrea Richardson:

An Adoption Diary

AT SEVENTEEN, ANDREA RICHARDSON MADE THE
HEARTBREAKING DECISION TO GIVE HER
UNBORN SON UP FOR ADOPTION. HERE, SHE
CHRONICLES HER STORY AS SHE FACES THE
CHALLENGE OF HER LIFE.

ANDREA RICHARDSON
AS TOLD TO GABRIELLE COSGROVE

M

Y NAME IS ANDREA RICHARDSON, AND I'D LIKE TO TELL YOU MY STORY. I'M SEVENTEEN, AND RIGHT NOW I'M LIVING AND GOING

to school at the Gladney Center for Adoption, an adoption agency and maternity home in Fort Worth. My baby is due the first week of May, and then he or she will be placed with adoptive parents. I found out I was pregnant last September. I felt so stupid. Pregnancy was the furthest thing from my teenage mind. Before now, I don't think anyone could've made me understand that this could happen to me.

When I told my boyfriend, he was shocked that I would choose adoption. We're no longer involved, and I haven't talked to him for more than three months. Then I told my family—my mom, Diane, my dad, Michael, his wife, Kris, and my brothers Jason, twenty, and Nathan, nineteen. It was the most awful thing I've ever gone through. I guess that's why I want to tell my story. Maybe a girl will read this and realize there are serious consequences to her decisions. Or maybe a pregnant girl will decide to give her baby the opportunities she wouldn't be able to provide. Deciding to give up my baby was one of the hardest choices I'll ever make. But I know it's the right thing: I'm not ready to be a parent, and my baby deserves a better future. So do I. I came here last October; in January, I started my diary for *Teen People*.

FRIDAY 1/22/99

I didn't know that anything could be this painful. I ask myself over and over if what I'm doing is right. Logic tells me it is, but that's little comfort to the mother inside me who just wants to be with her baby forever. It's a wonderful feeling to have this warm little life growing inside me. When I feel its little feet kick me, I realize how much I love it. Sometimes I feel incredibly sad—not for my child but for me.

SATURDAY 1/23/99

I can't decide what I want to give my baby to remember me by. Whatever it is, this will be all the baby knows of me, so I want it to be right. I was thinking of making a scrapbook about me, my family, my pregnancy and the adoption. Maybe a locket with an inscription, or maybe my own baby blanket.

MONDAY 1/25/99

Three of the other girls and I sat around my room, talking and eating chocolate. It's so nice to be with all these people who are going through the same thing. Our conversations range from constipation, sex and female anatomy to our feelings about pregnancy and adoption.

WEDNESDAY 1/27/99

One nice thing about this program is that I get to choose the baby's adoptive parents, so I should be getting Adoptive Parent (AP) profiles soon. There are still so many things I'm scared of: that I'll choose the wrong adoptive family—or that maybe I'm making a mistake.

SATURDAY 1/30/99

Yesterday I found roses on my doorstep. Apparently a florist donated two dozen roses to each birth mom at Gladney. I've never had so many roses at once. I don't have a vase, so I strung all twenty-four roses up on my wall to dry. I know it's gross, but I have been having the worst gas! Everyone says it's a normal part of pregnancy, but it is so disgusting. We've all lost our shame and embarrassment about things like that.

MONDAY 2/1/99

I talked to my mom. She knows a lot about pregnancy, and she helps me feel more comfortable with it. But she keeps mentioning having grandkids around. It makes me feel guilty, like she wants me to keep my baby, even though she says it's up to me.

WEDNESDAY 2/3/99

I finally got AP profiles! One I really like, because they seem to be very down-to-earth people. I'm nervous, though. The profiles make things more real. But I can't wait to meet my child's future parents. I feel like this is what makes all the pain worthwhile—being able to give a family the one thing they want most and being able to give my child the one thing I want most for it.

Andrea Richardson: An Adoption Diary

FRIDAY 2/5/99

I went home and showed Dad and my stepmother, Kris, my AP profiles. They had the same view on them that I did. But on the way home I started feeling really sad about how my life has changed and how I was going to miss my baby. I try as hard as I can to shove away my emotions about the adoption until I can deal with them. Right now, it's more than I can bear. I'm frightened that I just won't be able to go through with it. I wish that I could just sign my rights away now and get it over with, so that there's no room for backing out.

SUNDAY 2/7/99

My feet and ankles have been swelling so much. It's disgusting and uncomfortable. My tummy is getting so big, and my belly button is about to pop. My breasts are becoming big and painful, and I'm getting stretch marks on them.

MONDAY 2/8/99

It's a boy! I just had a sonogram. I got to see his little feet, legs and spine. I could see his little heart beating, and he kept opening and closing his little fists. I'm choking back tears. He has such strong little legs. I think he'll be a soccer player or a runner. I can't wait to see him face-to-face!

TUESDAY 2/9/99

I've chosen his adoptive parents, and we've met. They are so cool—they remind me of my family. It seems strange, but I'm actually excited about giving them my son. We talked about names, and I told them I wanted them to be at the hospital.

They already have a four-year-old son. He was so cute! He put his hand on my tummy and called it his baby.

Andrea writes in her diary—an assignment that would sometimes bring her to tears.

TEEN PEOPLE: Real Life Diaries

WEDNESDAY 2/24/99

I talked with Dad and Kris this weekend about how I'm handling things. It was the first time my dad really talked about it. He said having children is an indescribable feeling and that I have no concept of what a loss the adoption will be. I think I'll be able to deal with it. So many other girls do it, so why can't I?

TUESDAY 3/9/99

I haven't written in my journal for such a long time. I've been feeling run-down, physically and emotionally. My AP mom took me out on a picnic the other day. We talked a lot about our families, and we have a lot in common. I really like her. It made me feel a lot more comfortable with my decision.

MONDAY 3/15/99

I still have a hard time believing I'm making a little person, but I don't really think about being pregnant anymore. Maybe I'm getting used to it. I realize I'm making decisions that are going to affect my entire life, and it kind of scares and excites me. I feel like I'm moving further into adulthood, and I like it.

THURSDAY 3/18/99

I now understand better than I ever thought possible that it can happen to you. I guess there are some things you have to learn on your own, but the lessons can be awfully hard. I think back to when I first got pregnant, and sometimes I wish I was the kind of person who could just get an abortion. It would have been so much easier—but I couldn't.

"When I first got here I thought it was weird living with pregnant girls," says Andrea, in her dorm room at the Gladney Center.

MONDAY 3/22/99

We have classes on the legal aspects of adoption, grief and loss and post-adoption. It was scary at first, but now I feel more prepared, knowing everything that will happen. We got a copy of the papers we'll have to sign once the baby is born. It was really hard to read them; they're very harsh. I know some birth mothers change their minds about adoption, but I'm still confident in my decision. Boy, I sure miss that time when my biggest worry was the grade on my math test or what to do with my Saturday nights.

Andrea Richardson: An Adoption Diary

FRIDAY 3/26/99

Adoption is such a sweet-and-sour experience. It makes me wonder if all of us birth mothers will have a hard time adjusting to the lives we used to live. Sometimes I can see myself giving up and becoming very depressed, and other times I see myself using this experience to become a better person. I just can't predict what will become of me. I don't want to wrap my identity around this experience, but I feel like it's inevitable.

WEDNESDAY 4/7/99

I am so ready to get this baby out of me! I can barely sleep. I wake up five times a night. I got my first stretch mark on my belly, and my back hurts. I feel huge; I just want to wear a pair of regular old jeans again. I can't wait to be able to do the things that I used to take for granted. I have only one more month left, but it seems like an eternity.

WEDNESDAY 4/21/99 9:30 P.M.

At the hospital, they said I wasn't dilated enough and sent me back to Gladney. I wanted to cry. I'd gone through all that pain and excitement, and they said it was false labor. But by 10:30, the pain in my back was so bad, all I could do was curl into a ball and cry. I wanted to die. To help the pain, the evening houseparent at Gladney put me in a hot shower and told me to lean on her with my arms around her shoulders. I stood there for the next hour, scared and sobbing. They took me back to the hospital around midnight.

THURSDAY 4/22/99 EARLY MORNING:

The next few hours were a blur of mind-shattering, unimaginable pain. I thought it was going to rip me in half. At 2:30 A.M., my stepmom, Kris, arrived. I was so relieved to see her, I began to cry. Kris said to think of my pain as my final gift to my baby, and when I did, I found the strength to focus and breathe. But it still hurt like hell. They finally decided to give me the epidural [a shot to numb the lower part of the body]. Within minutes, the pain was gone. The rest of the night I lay in bed and talked with Kris.

8 A.M.

My water broke and I started to get frightened. Everything was happening so fast. I began to cry—not from pain, but because I realized my baby was leaving me.

I began to push, and twenty minutes later—10:16 A.M.—my precious son was born. He weighed seven pounds, fifteen ounces. It was so incredible! It was truly the happiest moment of my life. I cried tears of joy, which is something I've never done before. They cleaned him up, and then the nurse handed me the most beautiful, perfect baby boy I've ever seen. He lay there peacefully in my arms, wrapped in a soft white blanket. I'll never forget his little face. At that moment I felt a love I'd never felt before. I love him with all my heart, more than anything, more than life.

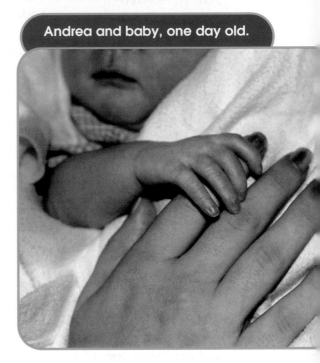

Andrea and baby, one day old.

FRIDAY 4/23/99 MORNING:

I hardly slept last night. I was in a lot of pain, and I just wanted to lie awake thinking about my beautiful baby boy. This morning, his adoptive mother and her four-year-old son came to visit. It was hard for me, but I let her hold him. When I watched her sit with my baby in her arms and her son in her lap, I knew I'd made the right decision. They left, and I spent the next few hours alone with him. I didn't want to put him down for a second.

AFTERNOON:

It was hard to leave the hospital without my baby. He'll stay with a transitional-care mom for a few days and come for visits at the center's nursery. As soon as I got back to Gladney, I began to cry. I've never missed anyone so much in my life.

SATURDAY 4/24/99

I recently learned how to crochet from one of the girls at Gladney, and I've decided to make my son a baby blanket. I don't know if I can finish it in time for his family placement on Tuesday, but all I did today was crochet and think of him.

SUNDAY 4/25/99 MORNING:

I went for a nursery visit with my mom, who flew in from a business trip in Seattle, and my brother, Jason, and his girlfriend, Brooke. I let everyone hold the baby, which was really strange. My family holding my baby: That's something I didn't expect would happen for years. My mom had to catch a flight back to Seattle and we wanted to have lunch, so we had to leave. My baby was crying from gas pains, and I hated to leave him like that. It made me so sad to see him suffer.

AFTERNOON:

Lunch was really nice, and I felt closer to my mom than I ever have. I could tell it was hard for her; I know she wanted to stay and comfort me the same way I had wanted to stay and comfort my son.

MONDAY 4/26/99

I signed my legal papers giving up all parental rights today. My mind was in a daze all morning. They made me sit and read the papers, then asked me questions to make sure I understood. After I signed, I felt proud of myself—I also felt a huge relief. It was almost over.

I spent the next few hours in the Gladney nursery, lying on the couch with my arms around my son, as he lay on my tummy asleep. I was exhausted. I nodded off for about thirty minutes, until his crying woke me. I fed him a bottle, and he fell back asleep. Not long after, the transitional care mom came to take him. I didn't want to let him go. Tonight, for the first time, I'm beginning to realize my loss. Placement is tomorrow. I hope I have the strength to go through with it.

TUESDAY 4/27/99   MORNING:

I crocheted till the early hours this morning, slept a little, then crocheted some more. I finished his blanket just in time, went to the nursery, wrapped him in it and held him close. My best friend, Hattie Linkenfelter, came to see my sweet baby, which meant a lot to me. And then, for the last time, I spent an hour alone with him. I could barely hold myself together.

AFTERNOON:

Kris arrived, and it was time to head over to the placement room. My whole body felt weak, and I didn't know if I could walk. I wrapped him in his blanket and held him close. I tried to control my shaking as I stood in front of the door, clutching my baby's warm little body to my chest, tears rolling down my face. I gathered my strength and walked

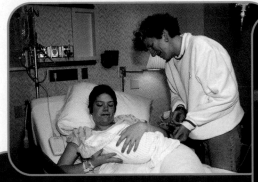

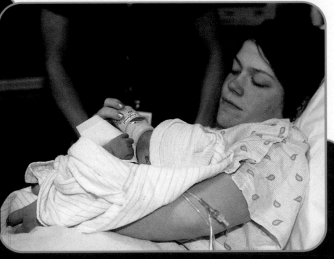

Left: Andrea's son, Michael Nathan, was born at All Saints Hospital on April 22. Andrea's Stepmom, Kris, was by her side soon after his birth.

Right: Just hours after the birth, Andrea cuddled and fed her new baby.

through the doorway. I gave him one last hug and placed him in the loving arms of his new mother. All I could do was cry.

Her son stroked the baby's little hand, and he opened his eyes and saw his big brother. His parents gave me a beautiful, heart-shaped locket. They told me that they'd decided to name the baby Michael Nathan. My father's name is Michael and my brother is Nathan, which is a nice coincidence. I cut off a small piece of Michael's strawberry-blond hair and put it in the locket. They told me that I'd given them the greatest gift, and that Michael will always know how much I loved him. I hugged them, and we took pictures.

Then I kissed Michael's forehead, turned and left the room. I felt that if I didn't leave then, I wouldn't be able to leave at all.

EVENING:

The day I had been dreading for months was finally over. I was a regular teen again. Kris and I went to the park and then to Chili's for dinner. We talked about college, relationships and the future. We looked at pictures from the hospital, and instead of crying, I laughed. I felt so great about everything. I'd given my son a life, and I'd given a family a new baby. Back at the dorm, I told the girls about everything, then went up to my room and slept for the rest of the night.

Andrea Richardson: An Adoption Diary

FRIDAY 4/30/99

The last few days I spent most of my time crying. Reality has set in, and the grief has been over-whelming. But I made it through the hardest day of my life, and that feels good.

SUNDAY 5/9/99

Today is Mother's Day. I opened my card from my baby's parents. It was very sweet and made me feel great because I know that Michael has such loving parents. I came home from the weekend, and my dad told me that I couldn't have handled things better, which made me feel great.

Above: On adoption day, Andrea's friend Hattie (left) visited mother and son. "She was in awe," says Andrea. **Right:** Finishing her baby's blanket meant so much to Andrea.

THURSDAY 5/13/99

I moved back home for good today. After living at Gladney for seven months, I'll miss the place and so many of the people there. It has been three weeks since I had Michael. Physically, I'm almost back to normal. I can fit into my jeans, and I'm slowly adjusting to regular life.

FRIDAY 5/14/99

Everything has turned out so much better than I ever thought possible. I still have good days and bad days, but overall I'm going to be fine. I'll be in summer school until June 4, when I get my diploma, and I'm applying to colleges this weekend. I think about Michael all the time, but now it brings a smile to my face. I know he'll always be loved and that he'll always know how much I loved him.

fast-forward

"Not a day has gone by that I haven't thought about him," says Andrea of the day she gave her baby up for adoption in April 1999. But she's happy that she made the decision to give him to a loving family: "There's no question that it was the right choice for me." She coped with her loss by throwing herself into schoolwork. She graduated from high school a year early, is now starting her junior year at Texas Tech, in Lubbock, and hopes eventually to go to law school.

For the first year, her baby's parents sent letters and pictures every two months. Last Christmas they sent a welcome gift—a video of Michael's first sixteen months. "It's awesome," she says. "He's crawling, walking. So whenever I really miss him I just pop it in and watch it." Now the letters and pictures will come just twice a year, so that will be hard. "I still miss him a whole lot. It never goes away."

But Michael's parents want her to be a part of his life, and plan to have the two meet when he is eight. "I can't wait, and I'm scared," says Andrea. "It motivates me, too, to really do well. When he meets me, I want him to meet someone who he can be proud to say, 'That's my birth mom.'"

Back home, Andrea still loves writing in her diary.

Andrea Richardson: An Adoption Diary

Moby:

The Voracious Vegan

MUSICAL SENSATION MOBY TELLS

WHY HE'S ALL FOR THE ANIMALS.

MOBY

AS TOLD TO LINDA FRIEDMAN

I'M OFTEN CALLED "THE BALD VEGAN." IT'S BECOME MY NICKNAME IN THE PRESS. AND YOU KNOW WHAT? I TAKE IT AS A COMPLIMENT—

especially the second part! I've been a proud vegan for fourteen years, since I was twenty-one. That means I don't eat meat or chicken or even fish (they have feelings, too). And I don't eat products that come from animals, like milk (unless, of course, it's soy milk) or cheese. As you can probably guess, you won't catch me wearing leather or fur. But that's not all. I also refuse to buy products that have been tested on animals.

SEEING GREEN

It's not always easy being a vegan. We live in a complicated world, and not everyone is as animal-cruelty-conscious as I am. If I'm on an airplane and I'm washing my hands, I don't know for sure that the soap hasn't been tested on animals. There could be thirty ingredients listed, and some of them might have been. But what scientists are starting to realize is that testing products on animals isn't just cruel and unnecessary. It's bad science. There are better ways to determine the toxicity of many substances.

So why am I a vegan? First of all, I've always loved animals. Growing up, I had cats and dogs and all sorts of different creatures as pets. Right now I tour too much to have any pets—it wouldn't be fair to them. But when I'm home in my Manhattan loft, the high point of my day is being able to play with my neighbor's pit bull. When I'm walking to the elevator and I get to stop and play with this cute dog, it just fills my heart with joy.

In high school, Moby was addicted to McDonald's and Wendy's.

During high school, a life-altering question which had been bothering me for some time started to really haunt me: How could I be so concerned about the well-being of my own pets while I was eating other animals at the same time? It just seemed hypocritical. I decided then that there was enough suffering in the world. I didn't want to be responsible for the suffering of animals. Intellectually, human beings and animals may be different, but it's pretty obvious that animals have a rich emotional life and that they feel joy and pain.

> I decided then that there was enough suffering in the world. I didn't want to be responsible for the suffering of animals.

It's easy to forget the connection between a hamburger and the cow it came from. But I forced myself to acknowledge the fact that every time I ate a hamburger, a cow had ceased to breathe and moo and walk around. In the United States today, we're extremely removed from the means of production of the food we eat. It's hard for someone eating a hot dog to make the connection that it was once the intestines of a pig playing around in the mud—if it was ever even lucky enough to get to play, that is. A McNugget may not look much like a chicken, but it used to be a sweet little creature walking around clucking and minding its own business. If people would just educate themselves about what goes into their mouths, I'm sure they'd change their eating habits. I don't think that anyone could go and visit a factory farm or a slaughterhouse and not become a vegetarian.

WHERE'S the beef?

Pardon the pun, but I didn't give up animal products cold turkey. Growing up in a Connecticut suburb, I had a pretty traditional (translation: full of red meat)

American diet. And, like a lot of my friends, I was addicted to McDonald's and Wendy's. But by the time I turned eighteen and moved into my first apartment, I was ready to become a vegetarian. First I gave up red meat and pork. I didn't really like pork much anyway, so that wasn't much of a sacrifice. And I'd never been much of a seafood fan, so that wasn't hard to cut out of my diet right away, either. It took me about a year to stop eating chicken. I can still remember the exact day that I gave it up. I was in San Francisco, and I ate a chicken sandwich that made me really sick. I'll spare you the graphic details, but in the midst of throwing up, it occurred to me that whenever people I knew got food poisoning, it seemed to always be from meat or chicken. That was the first time I realized that meat could be dangerous. (Now there seems to be a new article on its hazards every other week.)

> If you're considering becoming a vegetarian or a vegan, you should do some research first to find out which nutrients you need.

Within the next two years, I gradually gave up eggs and dairy products. Back then, I was still living in Connecticut struggling to make music, and I was pretty broke, so I wasn't exactly eating well. I couldn't afford a lot of the products in the health food stores. And I quickly found out that the stuff that's good for you often costs more. Did you know that brown rice is more expensive than white rice or that whole-grain bread has a higher price tag than white bread? I only had ten or fifteen dollars a week to spend on vegetables, rice, beans and tofu. I wasn't actually going hungry, but I got very skinny for a while.

Which brings me to a very important point: If you're considering becoming a vegetarian or a vegan, you should do some research first to find out which nutrients you need. This is especially important for women because they menstruate and can become anemic if they don't get enough iron. You still need to eat a balanced diet that includes whole foods and vegetables and the proper combination of amino acids. If your meal consists of white bread and mayonnaise, you're going to be missing out on certain nutrients. Come to think of it, if that's what your meal consists of, you may have other problems. Just kidding. But I know some people who become vegetarians and all of a sudden they're just eating doughnuts and bagels and cheese. That's not a recipe for a healthy life!

bon appétit!

Today, I live in downtown Manhattan, which is like a vegan's paradise. And I can afford to splurge at any of the twenty vegetarian restaurants and health food stores within a ten-minute walk from my apartment. I'm really spoiled. Yesterday, for example, I had all-wheat pancakes with blueberries and a glass of fresh-squeezed orange juice for breakfast. Then for lunch I went out with a friend and had a Mediterranean salad plate with hummus and tabouli. And for dinner I went to a macrobiotic Japanese restaurant and had miso soup, vegetable tempura and brown rice with curry tofu, and a piece of tofu cheesecake for dessert.

I can go to a regular supermarket and buy fake meat products like pepperoni, which means I can make a delicious cheeseless pepperoni pizza, and Canadian bacon. Even my meat-eating friends (yes, I do have meat-eating friends) think they're better than the real thing, not to mention much less greasy. I can also buy fake ice cream. My favorite flavor has a pretty silly name—It's Soy Delicious. But I have to admit that it really is delicious.

> **Ever since I became a vegetarian and a vegan, I've felt a hundred times better.**

My diet gives me more energy than you can imagine. The tour I just finished to support my most recent album, *Play*, was a year and a half long. When I perform, I run around on stage for two hours like a crazy person and get covered with sweat. If I was eating fried chicken every day, there's no way I could do that! When I was a teenager, my diet was terrible. I practically existed on fast food and soda. I was overweight, and I'd get depressed easily. I also had mood swings, and I'd often feel fatigued at the end of the day. Ever since I became a vegetarian and a vegan, I've felt a hundred times better. I'm thirty-five years old, and I meet up with friends I went to school with who have spent their entire lives eating meat, and they look ancient compared to me now.

living the
good life

Still, I'd never try to force my views on them or anyone else. I have some friends who are militant vegans, and if they see someone eating a hamburger they'll yell at the person. That just makes him or her feel bad and defensive. If I'm at a dinner party and people are eating meat, it doesn't bother me because that's their choice. I believe the most compelling argument anyone can ever make is just to live a good life and set a good example. My feeling is that I'm happy to talk to people and explain the reasons why I'm a vegan, but I don't judge people who aren't.

I will admit, though, that I think it's no surprise that some of the most interesting celebrities are vegetarian or vegan, like Madonna, Fiona Apple, members of the Red Hot Chili Peppers, and Drew Barrymore. There's actually a long history of smart, honorable vegetarians. Guess which famous scientist belongs to that group: Albert Einstein! He has a famous quote that human beings can't really be considered civilized until we stop eating animals.

Certainly I'd love to live in a world where everyone was a vegetarian and animals didn't have to suffer for human purposes. A goal of mine is to one day live on a big spread of land with tons of animals—a big menagerie of dogs and cats and chickens and pigs. But until that time comes, I just choose to live the way I do. Hopefully other people will see that it's ethical and healthy and some of them just might choose to live that way themselves.

Moby's dream is to live in a world where animals don't suffer for human purposes.

Moby: The Voracious Vegan

Jennifer and Donna D'Agostino*: Girls, *Interrupted*

SOME SISTERS SHARE EVERYTHING: CLOTHES, MAKEUP, GOSSIP. JENNIFER D'AGOSTINO* AND HER YOUNGER SISTER, DONNA,* SHARED A PAINFUL PAST AND AN UNCONTROLLABLE URGE TO HARM THEMSELVES. HERE, THEY TELL THEIR STORIES SO THAT OTHER GIRLS CAN LEARN FROM THEIR MISTAKES.

*Not their real names.

JENNIFER AND DONNA D'AGOSTINO*
AS TOLD TO DANA WHITE

JENNIFER:

I REMEMBER THE RAZOR EXACTLY. IT WAS SITTING ON THE EDGE OF THE BATHTUB, WHERE MY FATHER HAD LEFT IT AFTER SHAVING IN THE shower. I was drawn to it, like a person under a magician's spell. I picked it up, opened it—it was one of those old-fashioned razors—and removed the blade.

It felt very natural: pulling the blade over my forearm, letting the sharp edge dig into my skin. I felt nothing, as if I were in a trance. And when I saw my own blood, I wasn't scared; I was relieved. I wanted to see myself bleed. The blood leaving my body was like the pain leaving my body.

TEEN PEOPLE: Real Life Diaries

Six years ago, I was in the seventh grade and in a deep depression. I had one friend I hung out with all the time and a psychologist I'd been seeing once a week for two years. Otherwise, I didn't talk or socialize with anyone. I cried all the time. I'd lock myself in the bathroom, pretending to be using the toilet or brushing my teeth. But I was actually crying and looking at myself in the mirror and thinking about what a waste I was. I hated myself: the way I looked, the way my body looked. I needed to release this hatred somehow, and I thought the razor could help me.

I cut myself for a year. Little things would spark an episode—getting in a fight with a friend, or a guy being a jerk, or fighting with my parents. Just feeling like crap about myself. The number of cuts I made depended on how upset I was. Sometimes all it would take was a couple of cuts to make me feel better. If I was tremendously unhappy, I'd get carried away and gash my whole arm up. But cutting myself was only a temporary release. I'd think I was getting rid of all my problems, but they'd just come back again and again.

> I hid the cuts with long sleeves and Band-Aids. If my parents said something, I'd just shrug and say my cat scratched me.

I hid the cuts with long sleeves and Band-Aids. If my parents said something, I'd just shrug and say my cat scratched me. My parents aren't very observant. I didn't know it at the time, but my mother was struggling with depression, too. Her work, her family and fighting with my dad took a toll on her. She always seemed tired and stressed. My sister, Donna, didn't know, either. She's two years younger than I am, and though we're close now, back then we seemed like enemies, always telling on each other or trying to screw each other over. She was a kid, and I was going through puberty—that gross stuff. We seemed to live in different worlds, though I guess we were more alike than anyone realized.

Cutting myself wasn't the only way I acted out. Once I drank an entire bottle of NyQuil and hallucinated. Another time I swallowed a handful of Tylenol. But I don't think I really wanted to die. Maybe I didn't realize it at that time, but in the back of my mind I knew I could never go all the way. If I knew I had to take nineteen Tylenols to die, I would take eighteen. I think I was punishing myself for a lot of things. I had past experiences that had hurt me, and I was unable to deal with life. Hurting myself was my only escape.

When I was little, my parents fought a lot. They would scream at each other and my

Jennifer and Donna D'Agostino: Girls, Interrupted

dad would be, like, "That's it, I'm leaving." And he'd get in his car and we wouldn't know where he was going. I'll never forget the day he drove off and my mom said, "I don't think he's coming back." He did, but seeing that as a kid has an effect on you.

And there were other things.

DONNA:

When Jennifer was six and I was four, we were sexually abused by a teenage guy hired to baby-sit us. He touched us inappropriately, and he made me strip down and walk around the house naked. We were so scared of him; when we knew he was coming to the house, we'd hide in the closets and scream at our parents to stop him. This went on for about two months. We told my parents what he was doing, and they didn't believe us. Finally they said, "Maybe we should get a new baby-sitter."

Both Jennifer and I have talked to psychiatrists about this. They've told us there could be a link between the abuse we suffered and what we ended up doing to ourselves. The baby-sitter issue is out in the open with us. A year or two ago we even asked our parents why they didn't press charges. We asked if they still could. They said that it was too long ago and that we couldn't prove it, anyway. I wish we had pressed charges against him when we were little. Sometimes it just gets me so upset. Why didn't they believe us?

JENNIFER:

I don't think they wanted to believe us. Maybe we just took all the terrible things he did and turned all that shame and fear against ourselves.

Inevitably, my parents discovered my secret. One day I was sitting at the kitchen table talking with my mom. Earlier I had cut my wrists terribly—the worst I'd ever done it—and Band-Aids covered my arm from my wrist to my elbow. I was wearing a long-sleeved flannel shirt, and at one point during the conversation, I raised my hand. The sleeve fell, and I saw my mom's eyes bug out.

My parents took me to my psychologist. She strongly urged them to check me into a mental institution about ten minutes away. The hospital had a juvenile wing that cared for kids who had problems with drugs, alcohol and violence.

The next morning, my dad drove me there. My mom was at work and said she'd meet us. I sat scrunched down in the backseat in a daze, listening to my Discman. I was so depressed that I felt numb. When we walked into the unit, three girls approached me. One of them said, "So, what's your story? What are you? Are you suicidal, homicidal, a drug addict?" I was scared to death. I said, "Uh, suicidal, I guess."

The staff took everything away from me: my belt, my jewelry, even my shoelaces. Two hours later, after I was checked in, I had to say good-bye to my parents. As I watched them walk away, the reality of my situation hit me and I started sobbing.

All three of my roommates were sixteen or seventeen, so at thirteen I was the youngest. They treated me like a little sister. In the week I spent there, we bonded with each other; we all had problems, some of us more than others. One day one of my roommates, a recovering drug addict, went wild and started throwing chairs. Suddenly the words "Code Green! Code Green!" blared out of the loudspeaker. The doctors came running. They put her in a straitjacket, strapped her in the bed and gave her an injection. This happened to everyone in the room except me over the course of the week. Kids would just go off. All the kids in the unit knew what was going on, and we'd stand outside the room whispering about it.

But we weren't crazy. We were just a bunch of teenagers with really big problems. There were girls who sold crack, a kid who threatened to shoot himself, and a boy who got molested by a priest. The boys and girls were kept in different wards, but there was this community room where we could talk to each other. There was a red line down the middle of the room, boys on one side, girls on the other. But I'd just pull a chair up to the line and talk to the guys. Every day we had "school," but it was a joke: coloring between the lines and computer games. Most of the week was occupied by group therapy and private sessions with a psychiatrist. I spent the whole week just talking, talking, talking. My parents were really supportive. They visited me every day, but they never brought my sister.

After I got out of the hospital, things were okay for a while. My parents gave me a welcome home party, and Donna gave me a card. My parents thought the hospital had solved the problem, and it's true, it helped a lot. But it didn't heal me.

Going back to my old life was hard, and eventually the urge to cut myself returned. But my parents had taken all the razor blades out of the house, so I had to turn to something else. That

> Two hours later, after I was checked in, I had to say good-bye to my parents. As I watched them walk away, the reality of my situation hit me and I started sobbing.

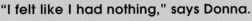

"I felt like I had nothing," says Donna.

Jennifer and Donna D'Agostino: Girls, Interrupted

something was a cigarette lighter that I used to light incense in my room. I was in the ninth grade by now, and one afternoon, after a particularly terrible day, I held the lighter under my wrist and flicked it on and watched the flame lick my skin. But just as when I cut myself, I didn't feel anything. The flame burned a dark brown circle into my skin. Soon I had a bracelet of scars, one on each wrist.

DONNA:

Jennifer never came out and told me that she was cutting herself. I found out from my parents. I approached her, trying to talk about it with her. But she didn't really have much to say on the topic. I just told her that I would be there for her if she needed to talk. It wasn't something that she liked to talk about, so it was just kept quiet. Maybe if we'd talked I wouldn't have started doing it when I was twelve. My mother thought that I would learn from Jennifer and not have the same problems. She was wrong.

> Maybe if we'd talked I wouldn't have started doing it when I was twelve.

The suburb where we live is like a bubble. Everyone's a clone of each other. If you're not like everyone else, then you're out. I was very self-conscious about my weight—I used to be a little heavy—and I felt like a fat pig. People at school would say something about the way I looked, or I'd have a crush on a guy and he'd find out and act all disgusted at the thought. I felt rejected. I had problems with my friends, with guys, with school. Everything just kept building up.

The first time I did it, I remember I'd had a really crappy day. I'd argued with a friend and was feeling really bad about myself. Then my mom and I got in a fight and I ran crying upstairs to my room. My parents had taken all the razor blades out of the house, so I found some cuticle scissors in the bathroom and cut myself. I thought it would be a release, that doing that would make me feel better. The cuts went away in about two weeks, and when they did, I did it again. I'd use cuticle scissors or a sharp nail file—anything I could find that would cut my skin.

I didn't really feel the pain. I'd make about six or seven cuts an inch long. I'd keep doing it and doing it until I drew blood. When it started bleeding, I'd usually snap out of it. I'd wash my hands with soap and water, then pat the cuts with my wet hands and put Band-Aids on them. I wore long sleeves and scrunchies around my wrists. I crossed my arms when talking to my parents.

JENNIFER:

One day, Donna came to me and told me what she was doing. "Don't tell Mom and Dad," she whispered. I said, "Okay, okay, just don't do it. You know what happened, Donna." She said, "Yeah, yeah, I know." I said, "Remember what happened to me. Don't be stupid." But I guess it wasn't enough.

DONNA:

I cut myself for two years. I'd do it once or twice a month, then more and more often, until it got to something like every week. But all that time I was in denial. I would tell myself, Oh, you're all right, you're better; you're not going to do it again. But I would. I never thought of the consequences. All I really cared about was how much pain I was in. I felt like I was at the bottom of my life. Nothing mattered. School wasn't important. My friends weren't listening to me; my family wasn't listening to me. I felt like I had nothing in my life, so I had to do this. I thought by cutting my wrists I wouldn't be in pain anymore.

In October 1999, I reached a crisis point. I was going with my mom to the store and I saw three of my best friends together. They had decided not to ask me to go with them. I was in a state of shock. After we got home, my mom dropped me off and left to pick up Jennifer at school. "Are you going to be all right?" she asked me. I said, "Yeah, just go." Then I called my friend and confronted her about not asking me to hang out with them. And she said, "Donna, sometimes we don't want to hang out with you." I got so upset. I hung up the phone and thought, I don't have any friends anymore. I have no one.

I went up to the bathroom, swallowed a couple of tablets of Advil, then cut my wrists. A little while later I took some Tylenol and lay down on the dining room floor crying. My mom came home and found me and cried, "What's wrong, what's wrong?" She took me to the emergency room to make sure I was all right.

After we got home, we had a huge fight. "I can't believe you did this. How could you do this to me and your dad?" she screamed. This made me feel even worse. The next morning, I didn't go to school. My mom made me keep the bathroom door open and made sure I was always in her sight. But I managed to get to the medicine cabinet and take twenty caps of Tylenol. Later we went to pick up Jennifer at school. I started to cry, and my mom said, "Don't tell me you did it again." After we got home, my dad was furious. He kept saying that he was going to "get me." It was a huge scene.

Jennifer and Donna D'Agostino: Girls, Interrupted

My mom drove me back to the emergency room. I just wanted to go to sleep, but the doctors made me drink charcoal to get all the toxins out of my system. I started throwing up all over the place. My whole mouth was black; I had charcoal on my tongue, in my teeth. I spent the worst night of my life in the hospital. My mom stayed by my side the whole time. The next morning I was taken by ambulette to the same mental institution Jennifer had stayed in two years earlier. I was still sick from the charcoal, and I cried the whole way there.

I was put in a room with three other girls. Two were drug addicts, and the third had hit one of her teachers. I kept thinking, Look where I am, in a mental institution. What am I doing here, what have I done to myself? I felt like such crap. I felt like nothing. Sometimes I wanted to cut myself, but they didn't even allow pencils in there. All I had to do was think about drinking that charcoal to snap myself out of it. I didn't want to go through that again. I just wanted to get help and get out of there.

The group meetings were helpful. I'd talk about how I was feeling and get everything out of me. I wasn't ashamed of it, because there were people going through the same thing. There were two other girls in my group who cut themselves, but they just sat there. I'd try to talk to them, but they kept to themselves. I felt bad for them. They were crushing themselves by not talking.

JENNIFER:

Once I went to visit Donna. It was really weird: We not only stayed in the same hospital, we slept in the same room, in the same bed. Visiting her was terrible. I hadn't gotten completely past my problem, but I'd made good progress. Being in the hospital brought up a lot of memories. The past came back and slapped me in the face, and I felt as if I was there all over again. Our visit was really awkward. I kept thinking, How could she do this? It was painful for me to see her, because I remembered what I went through myself, what I was still going through. I almost despised her. How could she? Why didn't she know any better?

DONNA:

My mom and dad came to visit me. My dad really wouldn't say anything. He couldn't believe this was happening again, that it was happening to me. My mom said, "I'm sorry that I never ever paid attention to you before this. I never meant to hurt you. I wish I could make up for it." I don't blame her. I told her, "Mom, this isn't something that just goes away. You have to remember this and you have to watch out for us."

After leaving the hospital I'd still get depressed, but whenever I'd get the urge to cut myself all I had to do was remember what happened to me. There are other ways to get through painful times, by talking, by writing your thoughts down in a journal. Cutting yourself or attempting suicide is just not worth it.

I haven't cut myself in more than a year. I'm on only one medication, an antidepressant; hopefully by next year I won't be on anything. I just take it one day at a time. Fortunately, I don't have any scars. I do have a whole bunch of new friends, and I'm doing really well in school. I've branched out, gotten more social, opened up. If something's bothering me, I don't keep it in anymore. My school lectures us about alcohol and drugs, but never about this. So many girls are afraid of it. But it's wrong to pretend it's not happening. Jennifer and I talk about it now. Telling our story together is a big step for us.

JENNIFER:

Last year in school, two of my friends came up and showed me their wrists. No one wants to talk about it. I guess I can understand that. People look down on you for doing it. They say they understand, but in the back of their mind they think you're strange and sick. I think depression is an illness just like cancer or diabetes. Studies have been proving that depression has a lot to do with your brain chemicals. There has to be some genetic reason that Donna and I both did this to ourselves.

I'm not sure I'll ever be completely cured. Every six months or so I'll get so hurt, so down, so depressed that I fall back into hurting myself. It's like having an angel on one shoulder and a devil on the other: Don't do it. Do it. But I've made a lot of progress. I can't beat myself up over it as long as I can pull myself out and keep working toward the future. I'm going to college, and I have a boyfriend I really care about. I was worried that because I couldn't love myself, it would be impossible for me to be in love with someone else. I still have my bad days. But there are also days when I look in the mirror and feel good about myself.

I think there's a reason why I suffer the way I do. Maybe someday I'll help people with the same problem. It's embarrassing when people ask me where the scars on my wrists came from, and sometimes I try to make excuses. But I can't deny them. The scars remind me where I've been.

Jennifer and Donna D'Agostino: Girls, Interrupted

Beverley Mitchell:

Growing Up on the *Small Screen*

SINCE SHE WAS FIFTEEN, BEVERLEY MITCHELL HAS BEEN LIVING TWO
LIVES: ONE AS A NORMAL HIGH SCHOOL TEENAGER, THE OTHER AS
LUCY CAMDEN ON THE HIT TELEVISION SHOW *7TH HEAVEN*. BUT WHEN
HER BEST FRIEND DIED, BEVERLEY'S TWO WORLDS COLLIDED AS SHE
DEALT WITH HER PAIN IN FRONT OF MILLIONS OF VIEWERS.

BEVERLEY MITCHELL
AS TOLD TO LINDA FRIEDMAN

M

Y WHOLE FAIRY TALE BEGAN WHEN I WAS FOUR YEARS OLD. I GREW UP IN SOUTHERN CALIFORNIA, AND I WAS "DISCOVERED"

by a talent manager while I was throwing a temper tantrum at a shopping mall. He thought I had a lot of spunk. He signed me up and started sending me out on auditions. Within a year I made my television debut in an AT&T commercial. Ever since that first job, I've always balanced going to school and being a regular kid with working.

The Fairy Tale's End

But there was a flip side to the fairy tale. In elementary school, when I'd shoot a commercial I'd only be absent for a day or two at a time. To the other kids, it was no big deal. It was just like I was out sick. But in third grade, I switched schools in the middle of the year to go to one that was closer to my mom's office. Right away, my new classmates started harassing me. They'd tease me and spit on me, and I'd get called into the principal's office because they'd blame things on me. It was horrible. I was the new kid who switched schools in the middle of the year. And I was an actress. They thought I was trying to show off when I was just trying to fit in. It's hard when you're that young, because all you want to do is have friends and play with everyone.

It got so bad that I used to make myself physically ill so I could stay home from school. My mom would have to pick me up—literally—and put me in her car in the morning. I'd be stuck in the fetal position because my stomach hurt so bad from being afraid to go. I ended up having to go to UCLA Medical Center for my stomach problems. And I had to see a psychologist, because when they say things eat away at you, they're not kidding. It turned out that I had torn up the entire lining of my stomach. After three months, I finally

Beverley realizes that being a celebrity comes with the added pressure of being a role model, a responsibility she takes very seriously.

Beverley Mitchell: Growing Up on the Small Screen

went back to my old school, and my psychological and emotional problems cleared up. But my stomach problems never went away. Once I got to high school, I had to take three pills a day, one before each meal, so I wouldn't feel sick after I ate.

A Dream Come True

It was during high school, when I was fifteen, that I auditioned for the role of middle daughter Lucy Camden on the TV series *7th Heaven*. Getting that part was a dream come true for me. I couldn't wait to start working. But I also loved my offscreen life, and I didn't want to give that up. So when we started shooting, I had an on-set tutor. But on my days off I always went back to my high school. I didn't want to miss out on anything, so my first year on *7th Heaven* I was also a cheerleader. There are a lot of actors who just do homeschooling because it's easier. It requires fewer hours and there's not as much pressure because you're not trying to keep up with kids who only have to focus on their homework. But I thank my lucky stars every day that I decided to stay in school. I have great memories from going to all the football games and dances. And I made some of the best friends a girl could ever hope to have.

DEALING WITH Private Pain in Public

What started out as one of the best years of my life, though, turned out to be the most tragic. My sophomore year, a week after we'd wrapped our first season of *7th Heaven*, four of my best friends were in a terrible car accident. It was after school on a Friday,

and they were on their way to see a baby horse that had just been born at another friend's house. The only reason I wasn't in the car with them was that another friend of mine had broken her arm two days earlier and I'd volunteered to drive her carpool for her. That afternoon I went to the mall with my friend Laura, and when we returned to her house her parents told us that there had been a car accident and that Kylie was in the hospital and Angela had died.

I couldn't believe what I was hearing. Angela and I had had an argument the previous week and we'd just made up the day before. I could still remember exactly where she stood on the school grounds and said good-bye and that she'd see me that night. There was no way I could accept the fact that Angela was dead.

That evening, all of my classmates went over to Laura's house to share their memories of Angela and to lend each other support. My feelings of grief were so strong, I couldn't even face them. So instead of dealing with my own emotions, I went into this hyperactive helper mode and ran around making sure all of my

> **There was no way I could accept the fact that Angela was dead.**

> I'm so glad we did that episode. I never could have fathomed the effect it would have on so many people.

other friends were doing okay. I was even asking people if *they* needed anything. It was the only way I could make it through that night that I wished was just a nightmare. For two weeks I stayed at one friend's house because I didn't want to face my bedroom, which had pictures and memories of Angela everywhere. That summer, my whole acting life was put aside to be a normal kid and heal and spend time with my friends. I put all of my energy into doing projects, like creating photo albums for Angela's family, which they still keep on their coffee table.

When *7th Heaven* creator Brenda Hampton asked me what I thought about doing an episode in which Lucy goes through the same experience of losing a friend, I was hesitant at first. I didn't want to inflict any more pain on the families involved. But after I checked with them and got their okays, I agreed.

In the episode titled "Nothing Endures But Change," Lucy's friend dies in a car accident after crashing into a telephone pole to avoid hitting a kid who runs out in the road. Lucy's supposed to be in the car, too, but she's late arriving at the pizza place where her friend is picking her up. She feels responsible and shuts out her family and refuses to discuss her feelings of guilt and despair with them. Finally Mary's ex-boyfriend (played by Andrew Keegan), who has also lost someone dear to him, is able to get her to open up and ultimately attend a support group.

It was beyond difficult for me to shoot that episode. It was a constant reminder of Angela and everything I'd been through. Just like Lucy, I'd had trouble letting my feelings out. In fact, I didn't really let myself cry until we did that show. For some reason, crying in character as Lucy allowed me to let my tears flow off camera. Once I started, I couldn't stop. I cried until I was completely drained physically and emotionally. And I finally started sharing my feelings. I found out that the more I talked, the easier it got.

It became clear to me that before then I had just been putting on my acting face. When I was at work, I was in Lucy land. It was an escape. I was putting on a show. But that's what I was doing away from work with my family and friends. I was putting on a show and pretending that I was fine when in fact I was dying inside. Looking back,

TEEN PEOPLE: Real Life Diaries

I wish I had confronted my feelings more directly. Now I know there's a better way to deal with difficult emotions and how important it is to talk about them.

I'm so glad we did that episode. I never could have fathomed the effect it would have on so many people.

Half of my fan letters to this day are about it, and I reply to all of them. I've received letters from people who have lost friends and thought it was their fault and were on the verge of suicide. They couldn't deal with their pain or put it to use in a positive way. Then they watched the show and realized there were other people out there like them who understood what they were going through. Just knowing that you're not alone in what you're feeling can be reassuring. I'm so thankful that I'm able to touch people's lives like that through my work.

By balancing acting with being a regular kid, I've experienced more of the joy—and pain—of life. I still think about Angela every day. I'll be walking down the street at the small liberal arts college where I'm studying film, and I'll see someone who resembles her, and I'll just freeze. But through my work, I learned how to deal with the difficult emotions surrounding her death. And though it won't bring Angela back, in return I was able to help other young people going through the same thing. Helping others helped me turn part of a tragedy into something positive.

Helping others helped me turn part of a tragedy into something positive.

Beverley has the best friends a girl could ask for. Left to right: Monica, Lauren, Jainey, Bev, and Ali.

René Stephens:

The
Stranger
Within

HOW COURAGE, DETERMINATION AND
AMERICA ONLINE HELPED ONE TALENTED
TEEN WIN HER BATTLE WITH SOCIAL
ANXIETY DISORDER.

RENÉ STEPHENS

I OFTEN DESCRIBE MY EXPERIENCE AS "AN UNWANTED STRANGER WHO KNOCKED AT MY DOOR CONSTANTLY." AT THIRTEEN, I WAS DIAGNOSED with social anxiety. It appeared out of nowhere and brought my life to a screeching halt. For four long, difficult years I would be haunted by something that I couldn't see or understand. It would be a long battle, but eventually I took my life back.

114

The stranger first knocked on my door in September 1994. A few months earlier my family had moved to a new neighborhood in Virginia Beach, about thirty minutes from the home I'd grown up in. I spent the summer hanging out with my younger sister, Lana, who was eleven, and brother, Taylor, who was nine. We went to the beach, swam in our new pool and jumped on our trampoline. Nothing out of the ordinary happened; it felt like every other summer before school started.

OVERWHELMED
by Fear

As September got closer, I enrolled in eighth grade at the local middle school. Almost everyone feels nervous and excited on the first day of school, but a month into the school year I was still experiencing butterflies in my stomach the minute my alarm clock went off. One morning, out of nowhere, I felt sick to my stomach and light-headed. My heart was beating extremely fast, and I felt as if I was going to panic if it didn't stop. I told my parents that I didn't feel well and wanted to stay home from school.

I went back to school the next day. I knew nothing about anxiety, so I thought that what I had been feeling had gone away forever. But I was wrong. Without warning, a full-blown anxiety attack hit me in class. The room started to tilt, and my vision was altered. I can remember clutching my chair, feeling as if I would fall out of it. I raised my hand and asked to speak to the teacher outside in the hall. I carefully exited the room and informed her that something terrible was wrong with me. I made my way to the clinic and ran straight into the bathroom, thinking I was going to throw up. I didn't, but I sat there, curled up in a ball on the floor until the dizziness passed. I was scared and didn't understand what was happening to me. I could feel my heart racing as if I had just run a marathon. I thought I had some awful disease, which scared me even more.

After that, the attacks started coming more frequently. Each one would last about ten minutes, but it felt like an hour. First I'd feel a sensation of "falseness," an

René Stephens: The Stranger Within

At eight, René was just a typical little girl.

As René celebrated her thirteenth birthday in August 1994, she had no idea of what was about to befall her.

aura that something was about to "go wrong." I would become faint and light-headed, and my heart would pound rapidly, almost as if I was having a mini heart attack. My stomach would knot up, and every muscle in my body would clench. An attack left me feeling physically exhausted and upset.

Going back to school became harder and harder. A lot of the kids had circles of friends they had known since elementary school, and I just didn't fit in. The kids would make fun of me because I missed class or I couldn't remember everyone's name. I was considered strange and weird. I had no one to turn to at school who could understand me, no friends—nothing. School became a place I couldn't trust.

What if I had an attack there again? I felt vulnerable and exposed. Just the thought of experiencing such embarrassment and humiliation would trigger an anxiety attack. My fear of feeling anxious in front of strangers eventually kept me from going to any public place—the mall, the movies, and especially school. The only place that I could relax in and trust was my home. It became my safe haven, and eventually I didn't want to leave.

I was scared of having to deal with anxiety forever—the mind of a thirteen-year-old doesn't go very far into the future. I felt suffocated by fear and pain, emotionally and physically, each time I had an attack. I could

What if I had an attack there again?

feel the presence of anxiety, the "stranger," everywhere. It was a lingering, constant worry that caused mountains of stress. I was beginning to feel run-down and worn-out.

As time passed, I went from being an outgoing teenager who loved spending time with her friends at school to someone who couldn't even go to the grocery store with her mom. I started to become depressed and my grades began to slip. I wanted to crawl in my bed and never get out again.

A PERSONAL Decision

By December, I'd basically become a hermit, never leaving my home unless I absolutely had to. My parents took me to a pediatrician for tests. My stomach was upset all of the time, and they were worried that I had an ulcer or a parasite. All of the tests came back fine, so they focused on my mental health. Thinking I was upset because I'd left my old school and friends, they enrolled me in my old middle school, but going back to familiar surroundings and old friends didn't help much. Finally, my parents contacted the local school board, and my guidance counselor suggested Home Bound, a program for kids who can't go to school because of an illness. I didn't want to do it at first because it meant admitting there was something wrong with me. But my body and mind needed a break, so I agreed.

A teacher came to my house every day to tutor me, and I had to go see a counselor at a mental health clinic every week to prove that I was actually ill. The first time I stepped foot into the waiting room, my heart sank. Everything was drab. The carpet was gray, the chairs were gray, the people were gray. I remember sitting there and staring down at my clothes, my hands, anything that still looked like me.

I had never been to a counselor before and didn't know what to expect. After describing my symptoms to my counselor, she informed me that I had social anxiety disorder. She was a nice woman, but she immediately wanted to put me on Prozac to help my "problem." My parents were concerned about Prozac's side effects—

René could barely make it to school by Christmas of 1994. "I'd become a hermit," she says.

headaches, nausea and insomnia. I didn't want it, either. My parents and I have always had an open, honest relationship. They listened to me when I said that I needed to find the strength to fight this from within myself, not from a pill. I wanted to come to terms with my anxiety rather than subdue it. We agreed that if this approach didn't work, we'd consider other options. My counselor abided by our wishes and never brought the issue up again.

In our sessions my counselor and I talked about everything from my feelings about school to my favorite movies, but when months went by and I was still experiencing anxiety, she brought in another counselor. He asked me if I was hearing voices in my head or if I wanted to commit suicide. They even asked me if I ever wanted to hurt myself or others in any way. I didn't understand why they were asking me these questions. I had never acted or thought in such ways. After discussing it with my parents, we decided to stop the sessions. My experience with counseling confused more than it helped me. After six months, I had gained nothing more than bad memories.

Inside
LOOKING OUT

I ended up staying on Home Bound for the rest of the school year and finished the eighth grade as an honor student. Summer rolled around, and the issue of high school came up. I enrolled, hoping that I could ignore what was happening to me and return to something that I'd always loved. But a week before school started, I suffered a series of anxiety attacks and told my parents that I couldn't go. I was confused, ashamed and depressed. I felt angry with myself, as if I was letting my parents and myself down.

My parents decided it was in my best interest to withdraw me from public school and work toward enrolling me in a home-schooling program. They did everything they could to support me. But I was often at home alone because my parents had work and my siblings had school. I would lose myself in hours of TV and endless thoughts, staying in my pajamas until after lunchtime.

When two o'clock rolled around, I'd stand by my window and watch other kids walking home from high school—a place that I wanted to go to so badly—and cry. My days were hard to get through, and eventually even going to see relatives became a nerve-wracking event. I was starting to feel terrified of people I'd known my entire life. I was depressed and lonely—my friends had moved on, and I thought that, at fourteen, I would never leave my home again. I didn't know who I was anymore or where I was going.

My depression came and went—I had good days and bad days—but my anxiety was emotionally draining for my entire family. What I was going through was new and frustrating for all of us. I tried to explain to my brother and sister what I was feeling, but they were too young to really understand. My sister was upset with me because I had stopped doing things with her. She was a member of the color guard team and begged me to come to her games. I never saw her once, and I regret missing out on so much by confining myself to home.

Safety NET

After a year, when I was fifteen, I enrolled in a home-schooling program called The American School of Correspondence. It is a top-rated program that has served students all over the world for more than a hundred years. After I began its college preparatory course, my depression lifted. I felt like I was "back in the game." Having my mind occupied and knowing that I was doing something good for myself kept me going. I had great grades and maintained at least a 3.5 GPA.

About this time my parents bought a computer, and it became my link to the outside world. I quickly learned how the Internet worked and started visiting health sites and educating myself about anxiety. I found message boards from other teens who were going through the same thing I was. I started spending a lot of time in America Online chat rooms; it felt great to have conversations about the world beyond my house.

In 1997, when I was sixteen, I became a fan of the band Hanson. The Internet had thousands of fan pages dedicated to their music, and some of them included fictional stories about the band. These stories sparked my interest—I loved to write and had always kept a journal—so I decided to try writing one. I invented original characters and plot ideas, and before I knew it I had written more than one hundred pages. I taught myself HTML code and created a Hanson Web site that developed a following.

During one of my late nights on the computer, I was logged onto AOL when an instant message popped up. It was from a girl named Laila Behzadnia who'd read my

AOL profile, which said I liked Hanson's music. Laila was seventeen and lived in California. She said she rarely met an "older" Hanson fan like herself, and we ended up talking. We discovered that we had more than music in common. From then on I'd spend three and four hours a day chatting online with her. It was like

Four years after the onset of her anxiety, it had become a way of life for René. She couldn't go farther than her front porch.

therapy. We chatted about anything and everything—except my anxiety. Eventually we started writing letters and exchanging phone calls, photos and videos. Her friendship gave me something to look forward to. When the phone rang, there was a chance that it was for me. When I went to the mailbox, I had hope of receiving something. She filled a painful void in my life.

A FRIEND
to the End

By the time I was seventeen I was used to the anxiety. I'd been dealing with it for four years and knew how to fight the symptoms and handle an attack. At least once a week I tried to leave my house to do something, even if it was just going to the video store with my mom. If I felt an attack coming on I would relax, stay calm and deal with it the best that I could. Sometimes I wouldn't leave the house for a month, but I was trying more often and getting better at it.

In August 1998, Laila flew out from California to meet me in person. Hanson was giving a concert in Virginia Beach while she was staying with us, so we decided to go together. I was ecstatic at the thought of meeting Laila and going to a concert with her, but a little nervous at the same time. I knew that if I didn't go through with our plans, I'd regret it forever.

I decided that it was time to tell Laila about what I had been enduring. The night before she arrived, I confessed everything. To my relief, she told me what a strong person I was and that she would support me and would do anything she could to help. I couldn't have asked for a better and more understanding best friend.

On the day of her arrival, I went with my parents to the airport to pick her up. When we pulled into the parking lot, the butterflies in my stomach flew right out the window. I waited

I'd stand by my window and watch other kids walking home from high school—a place that I wanted to go to so badly—and cry.

121

excitedly, and when Laila got off of the plane, we recognized each other immediately. She looked just like she did in her photos: She had long, curly brown hair, with eyes to match, and light freckles scattered across her cheeks. We were hugging and

Left: Laila, Lana and René enjoy one of Rene's first outings in four years.

Right: About to go see Hanson perform live, René, Laila, Lana and Taylor are ready for a night of fun.

grinning from ear to ear and we talked all the way home. The concert was a turning point in my life. I was never frightened or nervous, even though there were sixteen thousand people in the amphitheater. My brother and sister attended the concert as well, and we had a great time. We all enjoyed the music and even got to wave good-bye to the band as they left the arena in their tour buses. I let loose and was me again for the first time in four years.

I didn't experience an anxiety attack for the entire two weeks that Laila stayed with my family. To this day, I can't even believe it myself. It was as if she brought out the best in me. I had a companion, someone who understood me. We went to the beach, shopped and we got to know one another better. I became stronger in those two weeks. Laila was like an angel sent to me to give me the courage to take my life back.

The concert was a turning point in my life.

Waking Up

By the time I was eighteen I was out in the world again. My mother, who's a makeup artist, started working for a local TV show about antiques, and I interned there for six months. I met a lot of people, made friends and even appeared on the air a few times. I was proud of myself for coming so far and never giving up. I was beginning to feel like "me" again.

Today, at nineteen, my life is back to normal. I get nervous once in a while, but the stranger hasn't come back to haunt me. I still write for my Hanson fan site and am working on my own series of young adult books. I also design and maintain a Web site for the company my father works for. I've completed my home-schooling program and plan to enroll in college, where I'd like to pursue psychology and writing. I hope to someday counsel teenagers who are experiencing anxiety.

I battled my anxiety without any help or medicine, but that doesn't mean everyone should take that approach. Get help if you feel overwhelmed. Society has become much more aware of anxiety and other mental health issues over the past six years; there are even ads on TV to promote medications for social anxiety. Talk to someone you trust, whether it's a parent or a qualified counselor. You don't have to battle it alone.

If I could go back in time, I would hug my tired body and tell myself that it was going to be okay, that I would feel alive again. And I would tell myself to never lose hope. Every life has a purpose and a story. Everyone has tribulations and hard times. But when you realize that you are still breathing, that your heart is still beating, and that your eyes are still open, you'll know that what you're fighting will never win.

Today, René feels like she's finally out of her prison.

123

René Stephens: The Stranger Within

Aaron Carter:

Out of the Shadows and into *the Spotlight*

FOR AS LONG AS AARON CARTER CAN REMEMBER, HE HAS BEEN LIVING IN THE SHADOW OF HIS OLDER BROTHER NICK'S FAME. BUT NOW HE'S READY TO STEP INTO THE SPOTLIGHT—FRONT AND CENTER.

AARON CARTER
AS TOLD TO LINDA FRIEDMAN

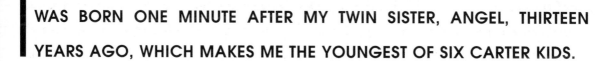

I WAS BORN ONE MINUTE AFTER MY TWIN SISTER, ANGEL, THIRTEEN YEARS AGO, WHICH MAKES ME THE YOUNGEST OF SIX CARTER KIDS.

My oldest sister is Ginger, a hair and makeup artist, and there's Leslie, fifteen, who's pursuing a singing career. Nineteen-year-old Bobbie Jean (everyone calls her BJ) is an aspiring actress and model. And then, of course, there's Nick. If you're reading this book, chances are you know all about my older brother. He's twenty-one, and he has been in the internationally renowned pop group Backstreet Boys for the past eight years.

As you can imagine, it was pretty crazy growing up around our house. And actually, it still is. My parents think it's even worse now! Back then, Angel and I used to chase each other around the house and have wrestling matches every night. Since I'm the youngest boy in the family, it's no surprise that I got picked on by my older brother and sisters. Nick was the worst. When I was around six years old, he got in trouble for throwing one of my Ninja Turtles in the ocean. My dad made him jump in and get it. I still laugh when I think about that.

When I was a kid, I idolized Nick, but not for the reasons you might expect. It wasn't because he was a singer or because he got mobbed in shopping malls. I was jealous of all the cool stuff he was allowed to do because he was older than I was, like play different sports (he's the one who taught me to throw a football), or go out driving around in his truck.

Wherever Nick went, I wanted to tag along. I actually met the guys in Backstreet before he did. Nick was late for his audition, and my mom and I got there first. I was only about four years old at the time. After Nick joined the group, I used to go to a lot of their rehearsals, and I'd stand on the sidelines, trying to imitate their songs and moves. When they started touring in Europe, I missed Nick a lot and I'd call him all the time. He'd always have gifts for me in his suitcase when he came home. At his concerts in Germany, he'd get tons of stuffed animals from fans, and he'd save them for me. It was his way of saying sorry for being gone for so long.

So what's it like having an older brother who's famous? That's a hard question to answer. Nick's been famous for as long as I can remember. I do know that because of Nick, our family got more attention than your average family. It was pretty common for fans to find out where we lived and just show up outside our house. It was always funny to me. I used to walk down to the gate, and they'd ask me, "Where's Nick?" I'd say, "He's inside. But he doesn't want to come out now." And they'd be, like, "Oh, my God! What do we do?" Some of them would try to climb over the eight-foot gate. We got our dog, Simba, a golden retriever mixed with pit bull and chow, to discourage them so they wouldn't get hurt.

Back then we lived in a city called Ruskin, which is outside of Tampa, Florida. (Now we live in Los Angeles and the Florida Keys.) Everybody always used to ask me, "Where do you live?" When I'd tell them, "Tampa," all the fans would end up driving, like, fifty minutes away from us. I wouldn't say Tampa to trick them, though.

I'd just say it because most people had never heard of Ruskin, Florida.

Seeing Nick sing had a big effect on me. When I was six years old, I told my mom, Jane, that I wanted to be a singer, too. She was really supportive right from the start. She signed me up for music and voice lessons and became my manager. The next year I formed a band with three guys from my music class. We were called Dead End. Looking back, I have to admit that we were pretty deadly—on the ears! I guess my voice kind of sucked back then. Still, we were able to book some gigs at local coffeehouses and libraries. Because of our ages, we couldn't exactly play at clubs. But one time we got to perform for around two hundred people at a music store in Tampa, and that was really cool for me. I knew I was hooked.

When I was nine, I recorded my first single, "Crush on You," which helped me land my first album deal with a German record label. My self-titled album was released in Europe a year later. Nick helped me out on the album by singing the background vocals on one of the songs, "Please Don't Go Girl," and cowriting the lyrics for another, called "Ain't That Cute." He also gave me lots of advice, including a great tip for performing in front of large crowds. Nick told me that if I ever got scared about the size of the audience, I should just blur everybody out and pretend there were just one or two people watching. Try it if you ever have to do an oral report or give a speech. It works.

By the time I released *Aaron's Party (Come Get It)* here in the United States last fall, I was used to performing in front of big crowds (my first CD ended up selling over a million copies overseas). And I was used to being compared with my older brother.

Aaron may be young, but he's got big dreams and is ready to make them come true.

The same thing had happened in Europe, so I knew it was inevitable. But the one thing I never got used to was being called Little Nick. You won't believe this, but sometimes my mom even mixed up our names. She'd need me for something and she'd say, "Nick, get over here!" And I'd be, like, "I'm Aaron, Mother."

I don't want to sound ungrateful, though. I know that I wouldn't have gotten where I am today half as fast if it weren't for the opportunities I was able to take advantage of because of Nick. Most new artists don't get the chance to open for Backstreet Boys. Nick encouraged me to sing, and he set a good example for dealing with fame (even though he eventually was able to buy fancy cars and stuff, Nick never changed). He also made sure that I managed to have fun. We've played a ton of practical jokes on each other on the road. I have a song called "One Bad Apple," and whenever I sang it, Nick, Howie, A. J., Kevin and Brian would take apples and bite into them and throw them out onstage. I'd be trying to dance and tripping over half-eaten apples. To get back at them, when they were sleeping, I'd take their shaving cream, put it in their hands and then tickle their noses so they'd smash it up in their faces!

It was a big accomplishment for me to finally step out from Nick's shadow. For the longest time, everybody knew me as "Nick Carter from Backstreet Boys' younger brother." There was no way to escape it. I knew I'd really made my own name for myself in the United States last fall when I did the Wal-Mart tour. We stopped in thirteen cities, and in each of them a huge crowd showed up to see me perform. The parking lots were overflowing with fans. After that, instead of saying, "There's Nick's brother," people started saying, "There's Aaron Carter." It felt really good.

Now it's Aaron's turn!

129

Aaron Carter: Out of the Shadows

PHOTOGRAPH Credits

Carson Daly: Soul Searcher
pages x, 2: © C. Taylor Crothers/Corbis Outline
page 3: © Monique Bunn/Retna Ltd., USA
page 6: © Bill Davila/Retna Ltd., USA

Ashley Rhodes-Courter: Escape from Foster Care
pages 8–9: "Family Tree": © Phil Courter/Courter Films and Associates
pages 10, 11, 15, 16, 17, 18, 19: Courtesy of Ashley Rhodes-Courter

Elisa Donovan: Starving for Success
pages 20–21, 22, 23, 27, 31: © Jan Sonnenmair
page 33: © Steve Granitz/Retna Ltd., USA

Jessi Ulmer: Cancer Survivor
pages 34–35, 36: © Michael Carroll
pages 38, 42, 43, 44, 45: Courtesy of Jessica Ulmer

Tyrese: Making It
pages 46–47: © Jan Sonnenmair/Aurora
pages 48, 52: © OCR – Kelly Swift/Retna Ltd., USA
page 53: © Bill Davila/Retna Ltd., USA
page 54: © Steve Granitz/Retna Ltd., USA

Laura Heldt: I Drove Drunk and Killed Someone
pages 56–57, 58, 62, 63: © Michael Aron/Michael Aron Photography
page 60: Courtesy of Pat Heldt

Anthony Colin: Survivor's Song
pages 64–65, 66, 71 (right): © Michele A.H. Smith (for *The Advocate*)
page 71 (left): Courtesy of Jessie Colin

Andrea Richardson: An Adoption Diary
All photographs © Lisa Means/LM Photography

Moby: The Voracious Vegan
page 86: © Rahav Cosi
page 88: © Jamie Reid/Retnauk
page 89: Courtesy of Moby
page 90: © Jay Blakesburg/Retna Ltd., USA
page 93: © Sonja Pacho/Retna Ltd., USA

Jennifer and Donna D'Agostino: Girls, Interrupted
pages 94–95, 96: © Peter Holst/Image Bank
page 99: © B. Busco/Image Bank

Beverley Mitchell: Growing Up on the Small Screen
page 104: © Steve Granitz/Retna Ltd., USA
pages 107, 109: © Ed Geller/Retna Ltd., USA
pages 106, 111: Courtesy of Beverley Mitchell

René Stephens: The Stranger Within
pages 112–113: © Tony Pearce/Jimmy Williams Productions
pages 114, 116, 118, 120, 122, 123: Courtesy of René Stephens

Aaron Carter: Out of the Shadows and into the Spotlight
page 124: © Rahav Cosi
pages 126, 128, 129: © Steve Granitz/Retna Ltd., USA

If you have enjoyed *Real Life Diaries* then we're sure you'll like receiving *Teen People* magazine every month!

- Go on tour with your favorite bands!

- Visit the sets of top TV shows!

- Meet real-life teens doing really cool things!

- See candid shots of the top celebs at work and play!

- Get the real scoop on dating, school, drugs, love and more!

- Keep up-to-date with the must-have CDs!

If you'd like a *FREE PREVIEW ISSUE* please call 800-284-0200 or go to our website at www.teenpeople.com

TEENS....TEACHERS....PARENTS

Celebrate teens and their achievements!
Do you know a teenager who has made a difference?

Teens today are affecting the world more than at any other time in history. *Teen People*® magazine and HarperCollins Publishers want to celebrate teens making a positive difference in their communities and in our world. Introducing the

TEEN PEOPLE COMMUNITY ACTION AWARDS

Any teen age 13 to 21 who has made a significant contribution to the community is eligible. No act of kindness is too small, no plan too grand. It could take place at school, home or the local hangout. It can be an act of courage or kindness. If a teen you know has touched one heart, or one hundred hearts, we want to know about it.

What to do: In 500 words or less, tell us about the teen who inspires you. Tell us about your community and how this amazing teenager has made it a better place to live. Send your essay, along with the family contact information of the teen to **TEEN PEOPLE COMMUNITY ACTION AWARD, HarperCollins Children's Books, 1350 Avenue of the Americas, New York, NY 10019**.

The Award: The teen whose story is the most inspiring and impressive to our distinguished panel of judges will win a $2,500 scholarship, a trip to the star-studded **TEEN PEOPLE COMMUNITY ACTION AWARD** Ceremony in New York or Los Angeles in September 2002, a 2-year subscription to *Teen People* magazine, and a selection of books from HarperCollins Publishers. In addition, the winner's name will be announced in an issue of *Teen People.*

Three 1st Prize winners will each receive a $500 scholarship, a trip to the awards ceremony in September 2002, a 1-year subscription to *Teen People* magazine, and a selection of books from HarperCollins Publishers.